WEAPO

T0268062

THE SVD DRAGUNOV RIFLE

CHRIS McNAB
Series Editor Martin Pegler

Illustrated by Ramiro Bujeiro & Alan Gilliland

OSPREY PUBLISHING
Bloomsbury Publishing Plc
Kemp House, Chawley Park, Cumnor Hill, Oxford OX2 9PH, UK
29 Earlsfort Terrace, Dublin 2, Ireland
1385 Broadway, 5th Floor, New York, NY 10018, USA
E-mail: info@ospreypublishing.com
www.ospreypublishing.com

OSPREY is a trademark of Osprey Publishing Ltd

First published in Great Britain in 2023

A catalogue record for this book is available from the British
Library.

ISBN: PB 9781472855961; eBook 9781472855978;
ePDF 9781472855992; XML 9781472855985

23 24 25 26 27   10 9 8 7 6 5 4 3 2 1

Index by Rob Munro
Typeset by PDQ Digital Media Solutions, Bungay, UK
Printed and bound in India by Replika Press Private Ltd.

Osprey Publishing supports the Woodland Trust, the UK's
leading woodland conservation charity.

To find out more about our authors and books visit
www.ospreypublishing.com. Here you will find extracts, author
interviews, details of forthcoming events and the option to sign
up for our newsletter.

Acknowledgements

I would like to thank Rock Island Auction Company (https://
www.rockislandauction.com/), in particular Danielle Smith and
Joel Kolander, for their kind assistance in providing photographic
content for this book.

Artist's note

Readers may care to note that the original paintings from which
the colour plates in this book were prepared are available for
private sale. All reproduction copyright whatsoever is retained by
the publishers. All enquiries should be addressed to:

Ramirobujeiro@gmail.com

The publishers regret that they can enter into no correspondence
upon this matter.

Front cover, above: SVD-63 with PSO-1 sight. (© Royal
Armouries PR.13074)

Front cover, below: A Hungarian soldier demonstrates the
textbook kneeling position for firing the SVD. He is increasing
the number of stabilizing points of contact with the weapon,
using not only his hands and the contact point between his front
knee and elbow, but also the tree to reduce lateral movement.
(LCPL. M.A. SUNDERLAND/Wikimedia/Public Domain)

Title-page photograph: This Ethiopian soldier on peacekeeping
operations in Somalia in 2014 is armed with an SVD. The
Ethiopian Ground Forces and the Ethiopian National Defense
Force have used both the SVD and the Romanian PSL over recent
decades; one way to distinguish the PSL from the SVD is that the
PSL magazine has a large 'X' pressed into its body. (AMISOM
Public Information/Wikimedia/CC0 1.0)

CONTENTS

INTRODUCTION

Can the SVD be considered a sniping rifle? This question populates the more arcane corners of the internet, and can produce a surprisingly lively debate on the part of firearms enthusiasts. To the layman, the answer might seem obvious: of course the SVD is a sniping rifle. It is a long-range, scoped-up precision rifle, capable of taking accurate shots out to ranges beyond those typically expected of standard assault rifles and battle rifles. The official Soviet military manual that accompanied the SVD stated a maximum *effective* range (my italics, to indicate that it is not giving merely maximum possible range) of 1,300m, the outer edge of its standard PSO-1 optic. Even the back-up iron sights are adjustable out to 1,200m. Given that the effective range of most assault rifles and battle rifles runs out at somewhere between 300–600m, the SVD must surely take its place among the sniping rifle family.

Not according to many critics and specialists, however, who make finer gradations of the military rifle family. For most among this group, the SVD is more properly a designated marksman rifle (DMR), certainly built for accurate distance shooting, but more for filling the range gap between assault/battle rifles and sniping rifles proper – the gap could be roughly placed at about 400–800m. With its semi-automatic mechanism, as compared to the simple but robust precision of a bolt-action sniper weapon, the SVD is a workable shooting tool for short- to medium-range point targets, but it is not the stuff of record-breaking kills.

This debate, it should be acknowledged, is not just a matter of ballistics and engineering; there is also a tactical and training element to be taken into consideration. In modern military forces, the gulf between a designated marksman (DM) and a fully-fledged sniper is both clear and strict. Both are defined by far more than simply the weapon they carry and shoot. A sniper has received the highest level of training in every aspect of long-range shooting *and* in associated tactical skills, such as reconnaissance, field craft and survival. Snipers might even act as forward observers for mortars, artillery and close air support. In their shooting capacity, they typically operate on their own or in sniper–spotter pairs, often working at distance from the main forces, acting as overwatch. A DM, by contrast, receives additional training in long-range shooting and tactics, but rarely to the exhaustive standards of the sniper. The DM operates in an integrated fashion within a rifle squad, section or platoon, rather than operating at some distance from it, and is called upon to add fire discipline and range extension to engagements as a 'force multiplier'.

Crucially, and in Western armies in particular, there is a further mechanical distinction between DMs and snipers, in that the former are frequently equipped with semi-automatic DMRs while the sniper has bolt-action rifle types. For example, Western military DMs might be equipped with the American semi-automatic Mk 12 Mod 0/1/H Special Purpose Rifle (SPR) or Squad Designated Marksman Rifle (SDM-R), the German G28 or the British L129A1. Snipers from those countries, by contrast, are more likely to be seen with bolt-action weapons such as the American M22 Precision Sniper Rifle (PSR), the German RS9 or the British L115A3. The reasons for, and the relative pros and cons of, semi-automatic and bolt-action sniping rifles will be discussed in this study, but for now we can summarize by saying that bolt-action sniping rifles have the edge in terms of long-range precision and consistency, while semi-automatics allow for faster follow-up shots but are accurate over shorter ranges.

I would agree that the SVD is more of a DMR than a sniping rifle, at least from a Western perspective. The semi-automatic operating mechanism, back-up iron sights, bayonet fitting and Soviet infantry distribution patterns all suggest the DMR mould – but perhaps 'Western perspective' is a significant qualification. Interpreted through the Western military labels of the last two or three decades, the SVD matches all the criteria of a DMR, but across the rifle's lifespan and its more-than-impressive list of users, the argument about DMR or sniping rifle can appear somewhat more academic.

The fact is that the SVD is one of the most successful precision military shooting tools of modern history. Like a sniping version of the AK assault

Two specimens of the SVD-63 on display at the Izhevsk armaments factory. The weapon on the left is fitted with the standard PSO-1 telescopic sight, while the rifle next to it has the 1PN58 NSPUM night-vision scope, a bulky instrument measuring 458mm in length and adding an extra 2kg weight to the weapon. (Vitaly V. Kuzmin/Wikimedia/CC BY-SA 4.0)

rifle it partly resembles (but is unrelated to), the SVD has had a hugely significant operational influence and widespread international distribution, and has been used persuasively by the armies or insurgents of more than 50 nations since its introduction in 1967. A selection of the countries that have used or continue to use the SVD includes Afghanistan, Austria, Burundi, China, Egypt, India, Iran, Iraq, Kazakhstan, Latvia, Mali, Nicaragua, North Korea, Philippines, Poland, Senegal, Sudan, Tajikistan, Ukraine, Venezuela and Vietnam.

Additionally, the SVD has been combat proven. Anyone within 800m of a hostile SVD operator should take proper tactical care – SVDs have killed untold thousands of people in conflicts ranging from the Soviet–Afghan War of 1979–89 to the Russo-Chechen wars of the 1990s and 2000s (during which both sides targeted each other with SVDs), and from the Sino-Vietnamese War of 1979 to recent battles between Russian and Ukrainian forces since February 2022. In these conflicts, the SVD has moved seamlessly between the DM and sniping roles, with kills being made at ranges anywhere between a few tens of metres to in excess of 1,000m, although the latter are rare and certainly might be more a matter of luck than judgement.

Perhaps we can see the SVD as something of an 'everyman' sniping rifle, approximating to the marksman equivalent of the general-purpose machine gun concept, with capabilities and roles defined as much by use as by design and build. We should also remind ourselves that however the SVD compares to other weapons, it still largely fulfils many of the criteria of a sniping rifle. A military sniping rifle has to be able to achieve a 1–2.5 MOA (minute of angle) accuracy, and the SVD can achieve this at about 1.5–2 MOA within its effective range, depending on a few variables to be discussed. Crucially, as we begin our historical journey through the development of the SVD, we will see that the Soviets designed the weapon with the word 'sniper' in its very name – its full title is *Snayperskaya Vintovka sistemy Dragunova obraztsa 1963 goda*, literally 'Sniper Rifle, System of Dragunov, Model of the Year 1963'. The fact that the SVD is still very much in operational use today tells us much about the success of Soviet efforts to develop a 'general-purpose' sniping weapon.

A pair of SVDs imported into the United States as Dragunov Tigers. The rifle at the bottom was designated as a 'hunting carbine', with a solid rear stock with no cheek rest, an unvented forend, no flash hider and feeding from five-round magazines. (Cas4j/ Wikimedia/CC BY-SA 4.0)

DEVELOPMENT
Innovation in sniping

The standard Red Army sniping rifle at the beginning of World War II was the scoped 7.62mm Mosin-Nagant 1891/30. This weapon was simplicity itself – a solid bolt-action infantry rifle that, when fitted with a 4× scope, was capable of taking shots out past 800m. By the end of the 1930s, however, the Soviet Union was making innovative strides in semi-automatic military firearms, and its ordnance authorities began to consider the possibilities for a semi-automatic sniping rifle.

The first to break this new ground was a sniper version of Sergei Gavrilovich Simonov's 7.62mm AVS-36 battle rifle, introduced into Red Army service in 1936. The AVS-36 saw limited combat testing against Finnish forces during the Winter War of 1939–40, but it was neither accurate enough nor available in sufficient quantities to take root in the Red Army. In 1940, therefore, focus switched to producing a sniping variant of Fedor Vasilievich Tokarev's 7.62mm SVT-40, which was already on its way to becoming the standard Soviet semi-automatic battle rifle of World War II. Minimal changes were made to bring the SVT-40 up to sniper potential. It was fitted with the 4× scope and greater attention was

Three Ukrainian snipers train at the Yavoriv training centre in Starychi, Ukraine, August 2017. Each man is equipped with an SVD-63 rifle, and the visible pattern of each forend suggests they are older models from the Soviet era. (Pierre Crom/Getty Images)

The SVT-40 was the Soviet Union's first officially adopted semi-automatic sniping rifle. Service life, however, revealed that the weapon was unsuited to the level of accuracy demanded of a sniping rifle, even though its effective range when fitted with a 4× scope was ostensibly up to 1,000m. (TopGunRMNP/ Wikimedia/CC BY-SA 3.0)

paid to bore quality, but otherwise it was still the regular infantry weapon. This fact showed in combat. The SVT-40 sniping rifle was notably inaccurate compared to the M1891/30, especially as the barrel warmed up from repeat shots. A total of 48,992 SVT-40 sniping rifles were produced in 1941–42, but in 1942 negative frontline feedback led to production being stopped and the focus switched back to the M1891/30 sniper variant, manufacture of which had temporarily ceased during the experiment with the SVT-40 (Bolotin 1995: 112).

This would not be the end of interest in the semi-automatic sniping rifle, however. In 1945, for example, Simonov developed a prototype sniping version of his SKS-45 carbine, in 7.62×54mmR calibre; but, like its predecessors, the required accuracy simply wasn't there. At the beginning of the 1950s, therefore, the Soviet authorities recognized the need for an all-new semi-automatic sniping rifle that was designed from the ground up as a precision shooting tool, not simply as a scoped version of a standard assault rifle or battle rifle.

Few other militaries in the world at this time were seriously contemplating semi-automatic sniping rifles (although they would begin to do so in the 1960s), so what was it that prompted the Soviet investment? During the 1950s, the Soviet authorities became aware that their infantry forces might confront, should the Cold War go 'hot', new generations of semi-automatic and full-automatic NATO battle rifles, chambered for 7.62×51mm cartridges that had effective ranges of more than 600m. The standard Soviet assault rifle, the AK-47/AKM chambering the 7.62×39mm cartridge, was superior as a short- to medium-range tactical firearm, but at the 400–800m range the NATO weapons would have the edge.

The move to design and adopt a semi-automatic sniping rifle was therefore an attempt to give the Soviet mechanized rifle squad a battlefield force multiplier at ranges equal to and beyond those of NATO firepower, including its machine guns. The semi-automatic operating mechanism could put down a heavier volume of precision shots, allowing for more rapid switching between multiple individual targets and greater chances of a scoring a hit on moving targets. Another motivation behind the new sniping rifle was that it could counter the first generation of battlefield anti-tank guided missiles (ATGMs). These typically had effective ranges of 200–2,000m, and the new sniping rifle would be able to target ATGM teams in the first 1,000m of that spectrum.

DRAGUNOV AND THE SNIPING RIFLE TRIALS

In 1957, a senior firearms engineer named Evgeni Fedorovich Dragunov was instructed to begin work on a new semi-automatic sniping rifle. Firearms ran in Dragunov's blood. He was born on 20 February 1920 in Izhevsk, home to one of Russia and the Soviet Union's great firearms manufacturing plants, established in the early 19th century. Many of his family members worked as armourers at the plant. Dragunov himself trained as an engineer at an industrial technical school in the 1930s and during World War II he became a senior gunsmith at a school for junior

Two close-up photos of the lower receiver of a Soviet-made SVD-63, this particular weapon having been produced in 1967. The upper motif cut into the metalwork is the Izhmash Arsenal cartouche, consisting of an arrow with fletching feathers in a triangle. (Rock Island Auction Company)

commanders. Following his demobilization in 1945, he took a position as a senior armourer at Izhevsk, designing sporting and military rifles.

One of the strengths that Dragunov brought to the SVD project was that he was a keen competition shot, so he invested the design with a shooter's understanding about what was important in terms of functionality and operation. The challenge to design a new semi-automatic sniping rifle had to negotiate a complex series of trade-offs, however. First, to ensure ammunition compatibility with other infantry firearms, Dragunov had to work-in the 7.62×54mmR cartridge, which required a magazine that would function smoothly with the old rimmed round. This challenge took much mental effort and also collaboration to fulfil – in Dragunov's own writings, he stated that the magazine design alone took more than a year (Bolotin 1995: 118) – and apparently he enlisted the help of a cooperative Aleksandr Konstantinov to crack the design (Forgotten Weapons 2019). The key areas of contention were precision vs reliability and weight vs portability. A precision rifle demands components that fit together with very closely machined tolerances, but a reliable weapon often has to have sufficient 'play' in its components to accommodate the intrusion of minor pieces of dirt and debris without malfunctioning. A highly accurate sniping rifle also tends to be a heavy one, on account of a substantial barrel (the heavier the barrel, the better it maintains accuracy as it heats up over successive shots), weightier components and extra fittings. The Soviet authorities wanted a weapon instead that weighed just 4.5kg fully kitted out, to ensure that the man carrying it had the same mobility as the rest of the squad – by comparison, a modern International Accuracy International AWM bolt-action sniping rifle weighs 6.9kg empty without the scope.

Dragunov evidently had his work cut out. In 1958, however, he submitted his rifle design to official weapons trials. He was not the only designer or weapon in the running. In fact, two other semi-automatic sniping rifles had been submitted, by two of the Soviet Union's leading firearms designers: Simonov and Konstantinov. All three designers had produced gas-operated rifles. The Simonov SVS-128-P.60 was certainly the more visually awkward of the three, with a solid rather than skeleton stock, a thick receiver, and an unusually deep gap between the gas tube and the barrel. Essentially an elongated SKS, it was the least satisfactory of the three, and its poor accuracy quickly removed it from consideration. The Konstantinov 2B-W-10 rifle, by contrast, had a flat in-line design and many of the features that would appear on the SVD: a hammer-type firing mechanism; ten-round box magazine; last-round bolt hold-open; back-up iron sights out to 1,200m. It also gave a nod to economies of production, using Bakelite plastic for the stock, forend and selector.

The main problem with the Konstantinov rifle was felt recoil. The in-line design resulted in a considerable kick from the full-power 7.62×54mmR cartridge, which the modest rubber butt plate did little to ameliorate. The recoil also tended to smack the user in the cheekbone (Forgotten Weapons 2019). Dragunov's weapon, by contrast, fulfilled most of the trial criteria, so it was selected to go forward for development and eventual production.

THE PSO-1 AND THE FINAL SVD PRODUCTION MODEL

The trial iteration of the SVD was actually known as the SSV-58. It was a simple design that was equally simple to operate – a short-stroke gas-operated firearm feeding from a ten-round magazine. Although the primary sighting instrument was to be an optical sight, the rifle also featured iron sights as standard, specifically a dioptre-type rear sight fitted at the rear of the top receiver cover, aligning with a hooded front post. Dragunov's own experience as a competitive shooter fed into this choice, as he felt that dioptre sights had enhanced usability over the standard U-notch iron sights on Soviet rifles.

The SSV-58 was selected to go forward to production, albeit with modifications. The final version of the rifle did not emerge until 1963. When it did, there were some notable differences from the trial rifle. The barrel had been extended by the incorporation of a prominent flash hider and there was now a bayonet fitting just beneath the front sight block. There were also changes to the iron sights – a more economical adjustable U-notch rear sight had replaced Dragunov's dioptre and there was a redesigned front post. The rear sight was also repositioned, now sitting at the back of the forend. All of these changes are likely to have been made at the direction of the military authorities, guided by their philosophy of making the sniper more integral to the squad while also making the rifle easier to produce.

In this format, Dragunov's rifle was finally accepted for production and service as the SVD-63. The rifle itself was only part of the story, however. Even as Dragunov was working toward the final SVD design, a new optic was in parallel development: the PSO-1 (*Pritsel Snaipersky Optichesky*-1; 'Optical Sniper Sight-1'). Although the PSO-1 entered production back in 1963, nearly 60 years on it remains a masterpiece of intelligent design, and effectively transformed the SVD from an adequate rifle into an excellent one. It is a 4×24 telescopic sight with a 32mm ocular

Left- and right-side views of the PSO-1 sight from the 1970s. On the left side of the sight (above), the knurled cap to the right covers the battery housing for the reticle illumination apparatus. The drums on the top (below left) and the right side of the scope body (below right) are for adjusting elevation and windage respectively. (Photos courtesy of Rock Island Auction Company)

sight, initially produced by NPZ Novosibirsk Instrument-Making Plant or at Izhevsk.

The PSO-1 has a range of features that might now be thought of as standard, but at the time were cutting edge. It was designed, much like the rifle, for the rigours of Soviet climate ranges and operational life, the body being filled with nitrogen to prevent fogging and to allow the scope to function across a −50°C/+50°C temperature range. One of its crowning triumphs was its reticle design, which featured a stadiametric rangefinder plus quick-access hold-over points for both elevation and windage, enabling the sniper to switch quickly between targets at different ranges and make lead calculations without having to adjust the elevation and windage turrets. With a 6mm-diameter exit pupil measurement, the PSO-1 had good functionality in low-light conditions, enhanced by the addition of an illuminated reticle option – the reticle would glow red via an internal battery mechanism. The sight also had a built-in infrared (IR) detection

A 1972-vintage SVD-63 produced at Izhevsk (in 1975 Izhevsk engineering plant became Izhmash Industrial Association). Note the extensive cut-out portions of the wooden stock, one of the principal measures taken to reduce the weapon's weight, alongside the lightweight barrel. (Photo courtesy of Rock Island Auction Company)

filter, which was a very advanced feature for the time. To charge the filter ready for use, the user exposed it to sunlight via a port on the upper side of the sight, with 20 minutes of charging equating to 48 hours of use (Dragunov.net). Once the filter was charged, the user rotated the sight's IR switch to activate it; this turned the sight's view a murky green colour, but revealed any IR signatures as whiter, glowing areas of light.

The PSO-1, unlike many other sniper scopes, was side-mounted on the left side of the SVD's receiver with a special dog-leg fitting. The practical reason behind this was that the bracket allowed the sniper to switch between the optical sight and the iron sights without modification of the rifle, a useful feature should the PSO-1 become damaged in action. The iron sights might also prove more useful if the sniper was compelled to engage close-quarters targets. All-round, the PSO-1-equipped SVD was a well-conceived weapon, with just enough sophistication to be competent in its sniping role, while being basic enough to fulfil requirements for reliability, weight and tactical function.

DESIGN AND OPERATION

Even when studied with a critical eye, Dragunov's SVD competently met the tactical and mechanical requirements asked of the weapon. It was a reasonably long rifle – overall length is 1,225mm and it has a barrel length of 620mm – and the weight is kept manageable: the empty rifle, without its scope, weighs just 3.7kg; adding a full magazine and the PSO-1 scope takes the weight up to 4.55kg (the scope itself weighs 0.58kg). The rifle delivers the bullet at a muzzle velocity of 830m/sec to a maximum effective range of 1,300m with optical sights and 1,200m with iron sights (these figures come with some qualifications, however, which will be explained in due course).

In terms of the SVD's operating mechanism, as stated above it is a short-stroke gas-operated rifle, using rotating bolt locking. (For clarity, in a short-stroke gas system the gas piston delivers impact to the bolt carrier

but is not attached to it, therefore the gas piston moves a fraction of the distance of the bolt carrier during the operating cycle. In a long-stroke gas system, the gas piston is attached directly to the bolt carrier and therefore both components travel the same distance.) The short-stroke mechanism, while more complex than long-stroke systems, reduces the felt recoil of the SVD by reducing the mass that actually travels backwards under gas pressure. Therefore the short-stroke mechanism is more amenable to a semi-automatic sniping rifle, in which quick recoil recovery for follow-up shots is desirable. The SVD also has a two-position gas regulator on the gas block, the regulator being opened to the wider '2' setting when the SVD has gathered some fouling from repeated firing.

A note in passing: while the receiver of the SVD bears a superficial resemblance to that of the AK-47 and its derivatives, particularly in the layout of the selector lever, the two rifles are not relatives, and share no common parts. The AK-47, for example, has a long-stroke gas mechanism, as opposed to the short-stroke mechanism on the SVD. Conflation of the two mechanisms has perhaps been facilitated by the Romanian PSL sniping rifle, which at a glance bears a strong similarity to the SVD, but is actually based on an AKM assault rifle operating mechanism, simply scaled up to fire the 7.62×39mm cartridge. Another key difference between the AK-47 and the SVD internally is that while the former has a rotary bolt with two locking lugs, the latter's substantial bolt has three locking lugs to deliver more robust and consistent locking. The SVD's recoil spring and its guide rod are integral to the upper receiver dust cover, which makes for convenient disassembly and assembly. Another practical maintenance feature is that the trigger unit can be removed as a single unit, released by means of a simple lever on the side of the receiver.

The operating cycle of the SVD is as follows. Prior to loading, the bolt carrier and bolt are held forward under the pressure of the recoil spring, the bolt being rotated into its locked position via the connection between a guide lug on the bolt body and a shaped turning slot on the bolt carrier. The three locking lugs are locked to the left into recesses on the receiver. The gas piston and driving rod are also forward in this position. Cocking

THE DRAGUNOV EXPOSED

7.62mm SVD-63 with PSO-1 scope

1. Butt plate
2. Butt
3. Rear sling swivel
4. Cheek pad
5. PSO-1 telescopic sight
6. Cartridge case (fired) in chamber
7. Rear sight
8. Forend/handguard
9. Gas tube
10. Gas piston
11. Gas regulator
12. Gas-tube latch
13. Barrel
14. Front sight

15. Flash hider
16. Bayonet-mount lug
17. Cartridges in magazine
18. Magazine follower
19. Magazine (ten-shot)
20. Grip cover
21. Grip
22. Receiver-cover latch
23. Receiver cover
24. Return spring
25. Return-spring guide
26. Bolt carrier
27. Firing pin
28. Bolt

29. Operating-rod spring
30. Operating rod
31. Magazine spring
32. Magazine latch
33. Magazine-latch spring
34. Hammer
35. Auto sear
36. Hammer spring
37. Sear
38. Trigger bar
39. Trigger guard
40. Trigger
41. Trigger spring

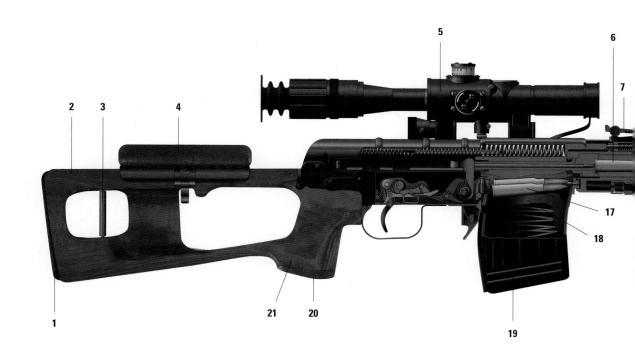

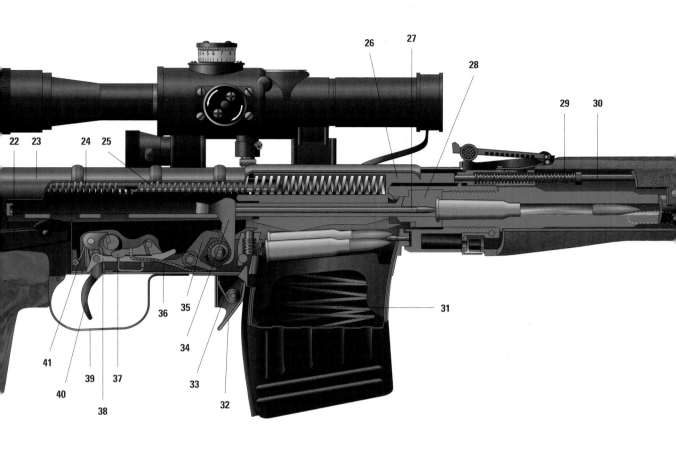

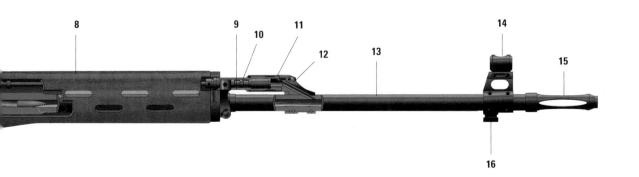

15

the weapon via the charging handle moves the bolt carrier and cams the bolt lugs to the right out of the receiver recesses, leaving the bolt and bolt carrier free to be pulled to the rear of their travel, and drawing the hammer back and engaging the auto sear with the auto-sear notch and the hammer-sear notch with the sear. When the cocking handle is released, the bolt and bolt carrier are driven forward by the recoil spring. The bolt strips the uppermost cartridge off the magazine and pushes it forward into the chamber; at the same time the bolt is rotated into the locked position and the bolt's extractor claw engages with the rim of the cartridge case. Also at this point, the hammer is now fully cocked, held in tension on the sear. The auto sear, however, is depressed by an angled portion at the rear end of the bolt. During the overall cycle of the SVD, the auto sear acts essentially as a safety mechanism, preventing the rifle from firing unless the bolt is fully in battery and the trigger has been released forward, an action that drops the hammer onto the sear.

When the trigger is pulled, the trigger bar disengages the sear from the hammer. The hammer flies forward and strikes the free-floating firing pin that runs through the bolt. The firing pin is driven onto the primer of the cartridge to fire the weapon. The bullet travels down the barrel and as it passes the gas port, propellant gases are tapped off and impinge on the gas piston. The gas piston is driven back a short distance by the gas pressure (a hole drilled into the side of the gas block vents gas externally once the piston has passed the limits of its travel). The piston in turn impinges on the driving rod, pushing the bolt carrier to the rear and repeating the process of unlocking the bolt and chambering a cartridge. As the inner parts recoil, the spent cartridge case is drawn from the chamber by the extractor claw and ejected from the right side of the rifle.

SVD SPECIFICATIONS
Calibre: 7.62×54mmR
Length (rifle only): 1,225mm
Length (with bayonet-knife attached): 1,370mm
Barrel length: 620mm
Rifling: four grooves, right-hand twist
Weight: (rifle + optical sight + empty magazine): 4.3kg
Weight of bayonet-knife (with scabbard): 0.45kg
Weight of bayonet-knife (without scabbard): 0.26kg
Feed: ten-round detachable box magazine
Rate of fire: semi-auto (maximum practical: 30rd/min)
Muzzle velocity: 830m/sec
Maximum effective range (with scope): 1,300m
Maximum effective range (with iron sights): 1,200m
PSO-1 scope magnification: 4×
Length of PSO-1 scope with eyepiece and eye shade: 375mm
Height of scope: 132mm
Weight of PSO-1 scope: 0.58kg

The auto sear is re-engaged. When the last round of the magazine is fired, the magazine follower engages with a bolt-stop, holding the bolt open so that the shooter can see his rifle is empty.

The SVD, while superbly conceived, was not a perfect weapon, and some elements of its design reflected the compromises made to balance weight, precision and functionality. Its barrel, for example, was thin compared to many other sniping rifles, meaning that as it warmed up from repeated firing it was prone to increasing shot dispersion from the point of aim (POA). The trigger was also comparatively crude and heavy, although in balance this meant that it was safer to handle within a mechanized rifle squad, where the squad members would be working in close proximity to one another. Overall, however, Dragunov had pulled off some masterful engineering, and created a weapon that is still going strong to this day.

AMMUNITION AND RIFLING

Sniping rifles only perform to their true potential when used with the very best match-grade ammunition, and here lies a fascinating but central part of the SVD story. At the time the SVD was adopted by the Soviet Army, there was basically only one type of military ammunition suited to the rifle. Known as LPS Light Ball, this cartridge fired a 9.61g (148-grain) spitzer bullet with a steel core. Although the LPS had punch and reach, in reality it was designed more for use in machine guns rather than sniping rifles requiring precision shot placement. In response to this limiting factor, Dragunov designed the rifling of the SVD for commercial sporting 'Extra' ammunition, which offered superior ballistic performance and accuracy over range. Extra fired a much heavier 13g (200-grain) bullet, thus Dragunov implemented a slower barrel twist of 1:320mm.

The problem was that the Soviet military ordnance authorities did not want to buy the commercial ammunition. Instead, they decided to produce their own cartridge specifically for the SVD. This challenge was given to ammunition designers Viktor Maksimovich Sabelnikov, Petr F. Sazonov and Vladislav Nikolaevich Dvoryaninov, and in 1966 the 7N1 cartridge appeared. The 7N1 was match-grade ammunition, with improved propellant and a lighter 9.8g (151-grain) bullet. The bullet had a full metal jacket and its core was two-part: a steel front part to act as a penetrator and a lead rear part to add weight to the bullet and to drive the penetrator forward. The shape was also improved, with a more pronounced boat-tail and a slight increase in the length. The claim, borne out in independent tests, was that the new round delivered accuracy 2.5 times better than the SVD firing the standard ball rounds (Fortier 2004).

The SVD now had a high-quality ammunition type produced from within the Soviet military industry, but the authorities did not stop there. They also specified that the SVD had to be capable of firing a far wider spectrum of 7.62×54mmR ammunition types, including tracer, armour-piercing and incendiary. The problem for Dragunov was that the 1:320mm twist rate was not ideal for these ammunition types nor the 7N1 cartridge, and in 1974 the Soviet military requested that Dragunov increase the twist rate to 1:240mm, which he did. This reduced the accuracy of the SVD over the longest ranges, but also improved its versatility. In the 1–3 MOA bracket, the SVD with 7N1 ammunition was perfectly viable up to 800m.

Looking forward in the ammunition story, in 1999 the 7N14 cartridge was developed for the SVD. This is an armour-piercing ammunition type developed specifically to defeat modern body armour, by virtue of a hardened steel tip. Bullet weight and muzzle velocity are basically the same as the 7N1, but during tests the 7N14 was able to penetrate 10mm steel plate at 250m, while the 7N1 failed to do so with any of the shots (Fortier 2004).

MODERNIZATION AND VARIANTS

Although the SVD was a fine rifle from the moment it entered production, over the next half-century it took several paths in terms of variants. Focusing first on the Soviet and, after 1991, Russian variants, there were actually some little-known experimental developments of the SVD that went barely beyond the drawing board. In 1970, Dragunov attempted to produce an automatic rifle offshoot called the V70. This featured a modified trigger, a heavier barrel, an integral bipod, 15- or 20-round magazines and a full-auto capability. Also around this time, Dragunov produced an assault rifle version of the SVD chambering the 5.45×39mm cartridge, with a shorter barrel, 30-round magazine, full-auto capability and minus the optics. The 1970s were evidently creative years, as there was also an attempt to produce an SVD variant chambered for a 10mm saboted round, firing a sub-calibre fin-stabilized flechette at a velocity of c.1,000m/sec from a smoothbore barrel. The weapon was designed to enhance the SVD's flat-shooting range and to increase penetration. It had an unusually bulbous flash hider and muzzle brake, and overall the weapon had very little recoil. As a subsequent alternative, the developer produced a version of the SVD in 6×49mm delivering an impressive muzzle velocity of 1,100m/sec. During the 1980s, a 'budget' version of the SVD was tested, using a stamped steel receiver and minus the long flash hider.

As much as these ideas represented blue-sky thinking, none of them were viable. The V70 convincingly fulfilled neither the criteria of a light machine gun nor a squad automatic weapon, the assault rifle was not required given the adoption of the AK-74, the flechette-firing gun could not deliver the required accuracy, the 6×49mm cartridge inflicted excessive barrel wear and the budget version was not structurally rigid enough for a sniping rifle. Thus these experimental weapons did not go beyond prototype stage, or not by much.

Where innovation did take root was in the bullpup versions of the SVD that emerged in the 1980s and 1990s. During the 1980s, the Soviets had experimented with developing a short DMR suited for handling within confined interior environments (aircraft, vehicles etc.) by airborne troops. Designer L.V. Bondarev, working for the Central Design Bureau

of Sporting and Hunting Guns, TSKIB SOO Tula, produced a bullpup version of the SVD called the OC-03, but its problematic shooting characteristics meant that it stalled at the development stage; plus the airborne forces opted for a rifle with a conventional layout. Yet in the early 1990s, the Soviet Union having been consigned to history, the bullpup idea was revived by the Russian Ministry of Internal Affairs (MVD), with the added requirements of a suppressor and flash hider. The new weapon produced in the Tula factory – the OTs-03 or SVU (*Snájperskaja Vintóvka Ukoróčennaja*; 'Sniper Rifle Shortened') – passed trials and went into production in 1993.

The OTs-03 was indeed an SVD in bullpup configuration (a long trigger linkage was visible on the outside of the weapon), with a barrel length of 520mm but a much-reduced overall length of 870mm. Other features included a collapsible stock and a combined flash hider and sound suppressor. Two years later, another variant emerged, the OTs-03A or SVU-A ('A' for *Avtomaticheskaya*; 'Automatic'), with the added feature of a full-auto burst-fire setting, the intention being that the weapon could be used as a squad automatic weapon in emergencies. The SVU-A's barrel was also shortened by 100mm and the flash hider/moderator featured a muzzle brake to control the weapon in full-auto mode, reducing felt recoil by about 40 per cent. Finally came the OTs-03AS (SVU-AS), stabilized by

The bullpup Dragunov SVU sniping rifle was a radical redesign of the standard SVD, in an attempt to create a compact sniping rifle for use by special forces and airborne troops. This is an SVU-A fully automatic version – the selector lever moves through Safe – Semi – Auto positions from the top. (Vitaly V. Kuzmin/Wikimedia/CC BY-SA 4.0)

A close-up of the suppressor and muzzle brake of the SVU-A. The maximum effective range of the SVU-A is placed at 1,200m with the PSO-1 or PSO-1M2 scope and the muzzle velocity is 800m/sec – just 30m/sec below that of the full-length SVD rifle. (Vitaly V. Kuzmin/Wikimedia/CC BY-SA 4.0)

INTERNATIONAL VARIANTS

The SVD has been adopted internationally on an extremely broad scale, and it appears under various different names in various different countries. In terms of licensed or unlicensed foreign production of the SVD, however, there are a handful of types that require a mention.

We should note that there are certain rifles which at a quick glance appear to be either copies or close derivatives of the SVD, but are different weapons altogether. The two primary examples are the Romanian 7.62mm PSL, which is actually little more than a scaled-up AKM assault rifle firing the 7.62×54mmR cartridge, and the Yugoslavian 7.92mm Zastava M76 and its Serbian update the 7.62mm Zastava M91, both of which have external similarities to the SVD but internally are again indebted to the Kalashnikov AK rifles. Then there are those weapons that blur the lines. The 7,62mm Al-Kadesiah is effectively an indigenous Iraqi copy of the SVD, produced by Al-Kadesiah Establishments from the 1980s until 2003. (Note that some of the rifles in the production series are labelled 'Al-Kadesih'.) The fidelity of the copy is far from exact, however. The Al-Kadesiah has a 1.5mm-thick stamped steel receiver, rather than it being machined like the SVD; and it has a receiver extension like the Romanian PSL. Other differences among a host of subtle changes are a non-adjustable gas system, a slightly shorter gas piston and the absence of the detachable cheek piece on the stock. Most of the Al-Kadesiah's parts, including the trigger unit and the gas components, are not interchangeable with the SVD. In reality, the Al-Kadesiah is not an SVD copy but rather a fusion of the SVD and the PSL. Iraq's traditional enemy Iran also has its own SVD-type weapon, the 7.62mm Nakhjir 3, which is essentially a direct copy of the Chinese 7.62mm Type 79.

Not an SVD, despite a superficial resemblance, but rather a Zastava M76, chambered in 7.92×57mm Mauser. Although they are different weapons, the SVD and M76 share the same tactical philosophy, the latter rifle firing from a ten-round magazine to an effective range of about 800m. (uzz75/Wikimedia/CC BY-SA 3.0)

A member of Iran's Islamic Revolutionary Guard Corps conducts an arms training session with a Russian-made SVD in a classroom at the former US embassy in Tehran, 25 September 1994. Iran has produced its own variant of the SVD, the Nakhjir 3, which is essentially a copy of the Chinese Type 79. (Kaveh Kazemi/Getty Images)

In the late 1970s, during the border clashes between China and Vietnam, People's Liberation Army (PLA) forces captured examples of the SVD from the People's Army of Vietnam (PAVN). Inspired by what they saw, the Chinese basically reverse-engineered both the weapon and the PSO-1 scope. The Type 79 that subsequently emerged was a near-perfect copy of the SVD, with the modification of the rifling twist to 1:315mm and a slightly shorter buttstock to make the rifle more comfortable to use by the typical Chinese infantryman. The Type 79 experienced some problems, however, largely related to metallurgy and production processes. The firing pin was easily broken, for example, and the cloned PSO-1 was disturbed by the rifle's recoil (Gao 2021b). The problems were resolved in an updated version in the 1980s, the Type 85, which also became the NDM-86 export model, produced by Norinco in 7.62×54mmR and also 7.62×51mm NATO/.308 Win.

Like the SVD, the Chinese SVD copy has undergone an ongoing process of modernization, divided between military types and commercial export variants. One of the most significant recent additions is the 7.62mm CS/LR19 introduced in 2014, which in many ways seems like China's alternative to the SVDM. Like the Russian firearm, the CS/LR19 has more advanced furniture and a top-mounted Picatinny rail for mounting different optics.

Two side-views and a close-up of a Norinco NDM-86, a commercial export version of the Chinese Type 85. The importer of this particular weapon was China Sports International of Ontario, California. Norinco also imported the SVD-type rifles in 7.62×51mm NATO. (Photos courtesy of Rock Island Auction Company)

an integral bipod that could slide forward to the optimal position just in front of the forend.

The SVUs are not the end of the bullpup SVD story. In 2013, Izhmash presented a prototype sniping rifle called the VS-121. This is essentially an elongated bullpup SVD with a heavy 622mm barrel and chambered for both the 7.62×54mmR and 7.62×51mm cartridges. It also has full-length Picatinny rails top and bottom for mounting scopes; the rifle has no iron sights, nor does it have a flash hider or suppressor.

The bullpup SVDs had limited distribution, mainly to government internal security forces rather than for military personnel. The military requirement for a compact sniper weapon for airborne troops remained, however, and this was fulfilled by the introduction of the SVDS in 1993. Produced by a design team led by Azariah Ivanovich Nesterov, the SVDS ('S' for *Skladnoy*; 'Folding') took a conventional SVD and fitted it with a skeleton metal buttstock that folded (when not in use) against the right side of the receiver and a separate pistol grip. The plastic cheek pad on the stock could also rotate to allow the user to switch more easily between the mounted optic and the iron sights. The pistol grip and forend were of synthetic plastic, rather than the traditional wood or Bakelite. The barrel was significantly shortened, at first to 620mm then to 565mm, and was thicker as well as shorter, with a stubby flash hider. The bayonet lug was also omitted. The receiver was redesigned, being thicker in profile and with some external differences. Standard SVD magazines were used in the SVDS, although later a polymer variant was introduced.

The 1990s also saw the SVD produced in a new commercial variant, intended for hunting and target shooting. To cater for a variety of customer requirements, the rifle was offered in three calibres (with different barrel lengths) – 7.62×54mmR (530mm), 7.62×51mm/.308 Win (565mm) and 9.3×64mm (565mm) Brenneke – plus a selection of buttstock styles ranging from solid wood to folding skeleton. Being sporting rather than military weapons, the flash hider is shorter. Magazine capacities are five or ten rounds. From 1993, these rifles were imported into the United States in 7.62×51mm/.308 Win as the Dragunov 'Tiger'. Differences between the military rifles and the Tiger are that the latter rifle has no adjustable gas regulator, no cheek pad on the stock, a muzzle often without a flash hider (although some imports did include this feature), a

Although thoroughly modernized compared to the SVD, the SVDS ultimately did not break away from the side-mounted PSO-1 scope configuration. It did, however, drop the bayonet-knife fitting beneath the muzzle. With the skeleton stock folded, the SVDS measures just 815mm in length. (Vitaly V. Kuzmin/ Wikimedia/CC BY-SA 4.0)

A side-view of the receiver of the SVDS rifle, fitted with the 4×24 PSO-1M2 scope. The lever just to the left of the selector, when swung downwards, frees the top receiver cover for weapon disassembly. (Michal Maňas/Wikimedia/CC BY 2.5)

simple blade sight (as opposed to a hooded sight) and a rear iron sight adjusted up to 300m, rather than the sniping rifle's long-range 1,200m. To conform with regulations issued by the Bureau of Alcohol, Tobacco, and Firearms (ATF) the US Tiger rifles also had the auto sear removed, replaced by a different form of disconnector. Tigers have been exported to other countries around the world, with subtle differences in design.

Also in the 1990s, the Russian military observed Western efforts to produce extremely powerful long-range sniping weapons in calibres such as .338 Lapua Magnum, and tried to find cost-effective means by which to give the SVD some type of parity, as well as better penetration against body armour. The result of this work in the 2000s was the SVDK ('K' for *Krupnokalibernaya*; 'Large-Calibre'), chambered in the 9.3×64mm option offered for the Tiger, albeit with improvements in bullet design and fitted with a more powerful scope and an integral bipod under the forend. The SVDK did not seem destined to become anything more than an interesting test in 2006, but it has subsequently seen service in the war in Ukraine.

The final iteration of the Russian SVD, at least at the time of writing, came in 2015 with the SVDM ('M' for *Modernizirovannaya*; 'Modernized'). The primary motivation behind this variant was the need to mount different, more powerful optics than the PSO-1 on the SVD, and the fact that the SVD was constrained to do so by its dog-leg side-mount system. SVD optics had already diversified since the 1960s. The PSO-1M

This SVDS, on display at a military exhibition in 2016, has received a modular forend accessory that enables the weapon to take alternative scopes on the upper mounting rails. Although the latest scopes offer some optical and tactical advantages, the PSO-1 is still a workable piece of combat equipment. (Vitaly V. Kuzmin/Wikimedia/CC BY-SA 4.0)

is essentially the PSO-1, but no longer with the infrared detector. The Belomo concern in Byelorussia (now Belarus) manufactured a version – essentially a copy – of the PSO-1 called the POSP4×24 and also produced the larger and more powerful POSP8×42, and even a 10× type (Dragunov. net). Belomo also produced the 1P-21 PO3-9×42 and PO4-12×42 Minuta sniper scope, which had zoomable magnification and automatic bullet drop compensation (BDC). The 1P-21, following good results during combat testing in Afghanistan, was actually adopted by the Soviet Army in 1989. These scopes are easily recognizable because they sit higher and more to the left than the standard PSO-1.

There were also two night-vision optics available for the SVD. The first-generation iteration was the 1PN58 NSPUM, a 3.5× passive image-intensifying device (i.e. it does not rely on an infrared light source) with a maximum range to identify soldiers of 400m, 600m to identify armour. The 1PN58 was issued during the 1970s and could be fitted on any weapon with a suitable mount. It was a very bulky addition to the SVD, however. The second-generation device, the 1PN-51 Improved Night Vision Device, was shorter and less ungainly. It delivered better resolution and visual clarity, with less of the blurring and distortion of the 1PN58. It also included features such as an automatic brightness control and a mechanism for protecting the user's eye from sudden surges of bright light. A subsequent sub-variant, the 1PN51-2, had a modified range-finding reticle and a much-improved mounting bracket.

Turning momentarily away from optics and back to rifles, the SVDM changes were sufficient enough to make it appear an almost entirely different rifle. They included a thicker and heavier barrel measuring 550mm in length, a redesigned folding skeleton stock with adjustable heel and removable cheek riser, a more ergonomic pistol grip (no longer an integral part of the stock), a compact flash hider and a redesigned top receiver cover. All the furniture of the SVDM is now plastic – gone are the days of wood. The SVDM can accept a detachable bipod that connects under the forend and the muzzle can also take a suppressor. Most significant of the changes, however, is the loss of the dog-leg side-mount

system in favour of an integrated length of Picatinny rail on the top of the receiver. This means that the SVDM can mount any optic of the user's choosing, thus increasing the weapon's tactical flexibility and performance over range and in different light conditions. The standard Russian military optic for the SVDM today is the variable-power 1P88-4 telescopic sight, which goes up to 12× magnification, although the venerable PSO-1 remains in manufacture and service globally.

Firearms specialist Vladimir Onokoy, writing for *Small Arms Review* in 2021, reflected on whether the SVDM is actually 'the last of the Dragunovs' (Onokoy 2021). From the Russian perspective, this is quite possibly so, especially with the adoption of the Chukavin SVCh (see the Impact chapter below); but the flexibility of the SVDM platform, with its capability to take all manner of optical devices and accessories, has given the SVD something of the 'modular' capability characteristic of modern military firearms, delivering what could be a significant extension to the weapon's evolutionary lifespan.

The SVDM is a radical modernization of the SVD rifle in every aspect – material construction, ergonomics, tactical accessories, sighting and other features. While the SVDM has certainly extended the life of the SVD, the fact that the modernized rifle still fires the now-ageing 7.62×54mmR cartridge may limit its commercial impact. (Vitaly V. Kuzmin/Wikimedia/CC BY-SA 4.0)

USE
Sniping on semi-automatic

Armed with an SVD, an Iraqi pro-government sniper takes aim from the prone position during fighting with Islamic State (IS) group fighters on the eastern outskirts of Ramadi, the capital of Anbar province, on 31 January 2016. (AHMAD AL-RUBAYE/AFP via Getty Images)

The SVD is characterized by some of the common elements that informed Soviet firearms design – simplicity of operation, rugged construction and practicality of maintenance. Now we move on to evaluate the SVD in terms of its handling and shooting characteristics across operational contexts and a spectrum of Cold War and post-Soviet conflicts. The historical journey of the SVD has been a colourful one. It has achieved huge distribution success, not only in terms of mainstream military adoption, but also through the shadowy channels of illegal sales. Thus while many Western sniping weapons are almost exclusively seen only in the hands of highly trained professionals, the SVD has been fired by the most eclectic warriors, from Soviet Spetsnaz special forces down to teenaged insurgents with the most rudimentary on-the-job combat experience. History has therefore provided the most varied laboratory in which to test the SVD's capabilities.

KIT AND EQUIPMENT

Before we go into conflict-specific settings, however, it is worth orientating ourselves to handling the SVD. The official Soviet manual that accompanied the SVD explained in detail how the weapon was meant to be carried, maintained and operated. It is a therefore useful not only to understand the fundamentals of the SVD as an instrument of war, but also because it opens a window onto Soviet military culture at the time. This in turn gives us additional perspectives from which to evaluate the weapon, as much from what the manual doesn't say as from what it does.

The core elements of the Soviet SVD sniper's kit were the rifle itself and the PSO-1 optical sight. These two were, however, supported by a

range of maintenance and functional items. First, the PSO-1 was accompanied by the winter reticule illumination apparatus, a battery-powered system to illuminate the sight reticle in low-light or night-time conditions. The apparatus also had a protective aspect in winter, the SVD manual stating that the system had to be used in temperatures lower than 2°C. The unit consisted of a battery case connected to a power cap via a long braided cord. To deliver the warming and illuminating energy to the reticle, the sniper simply fitted a battery into the battery case and then plugged the cap into the relevant port on the side of the PSO-1. As a bit of practical guidance about how to do this, the manual recommended that the sniper carry the battery case in the pocket of his fatigues or greatcoat and run the cable through the left sleeve of his outer clothing, thus ensuring that the cable would be kept safely under control while the apparatus was plugged into the optical sight.

The real oddity of the SVD was the fact that it came with a bayonet-knife and a bayonet fitting located under the muzzle. The SVD manual made it clear that the purpose of the bayonet was the same as that of any other rifle: to defeat an enemy soldier in close-quarter battle. Bayonet fittings on sniping rifles are almost unheard of since World War II, and with good reason. Not only does a bayonet, when fitted, affect a rifle's point of impact, but using one in combat would risk damage to the rifle's optical set-up and components. Such delicate considerations, for the Soviets, were largely beside the point, not least ideologically. Although the SVD operator was a sniper, there was to be no unaligned independence here. The sniper was part of the squad and as such was expected to get his hands dirty when needed, including participating in his unit's bayonet charges.

The bayonet-knife and its associated scabbard did, however, have a range of other functions acknowledged in the SVD manual, including as a hand-held combat knife, a saw, a wire-cutter and a general utility tool. There were two production variants of the bayonet-knife, defined by the manual as an early production model and a late production model.

This original Soviet-issue SVD kit consists of the rifle in its case (at the back), an NSP-3 night-vision scope with its metal box, the multi-pocket bag for magazines and the PSO-1 optical sight, plus a magazine lying on top of the bag. The Soviet-issue SVD bag held four magazines and the PSO-1 optical sight. The magazines, if filled, would give the sniper 40 rounds of ready shots, but he would typically have more magazines available for a combat mission. He might also carry 20-round cardboard cartons of loose rounds. (Photo courtesy of Rock Island Auction Company)

A Soviet-era SVD-63 from Izhevsk Arsenal, including the distinctive bayonet-knife and scabbard. Clearly visible is the hole through the bayonet-knife blade and the corresponding lug on the scabbard, enabling the two to fit together and hinge in wire-cutting mode. (Photo courtesy of Rock Island Auction Company)

The differences between the two mainly lay in minor details of handle construction, but the two blades largely shared common features. In addition to the main cutting edge, these included a top-edge saw blade and a mid-blade hole that engaged with a lug on the scabbard, the two pieces together forming a hinged wire-cutter. Early production scabbards also featured a rubber end-piece for the user to grip as protection when cutting electrical wire, although later scabbards had an all-over non-conductive plastic design. Fitting the bayonet-knife to the SVD involved sliding the mounting ring (which also formed a cross guard) over the flash hider, a clip on the handle engaging with lugs on the underside of the front-sight base.

We should note that some firearms authorities have suggest that fitting the bayonet-knife to the SVD could actually *improve* the accuracy of the rifle by stabilizing the barrel harmonics through the extra weight at the front. According to other sources, this was true when the SVD was used with the 7N1 cartridge (discussed below). The author has been unable to find scientific data to confirm this, however, but it remains an interesting possibility (Walter 2017; Thompson 2022).

The properly issued Soviet SVD came with a full set of maintenance accessories, contained within a dedicated pouch. These included a three-section screw-connected cleaning rod. One of the sections had a threaded head for taking the combination tool while another was threaded for the jag or bore brush; this section also included a slot into which a cleaning patch could be inserted. The third section of the cleaning rod was simply used to extend the length of another section. There was also the jag, a piece that screwed onto the cleaning rod and was used in conjunction with a patch to clean, dry or oil the bore, and a spiral nylon cleaning

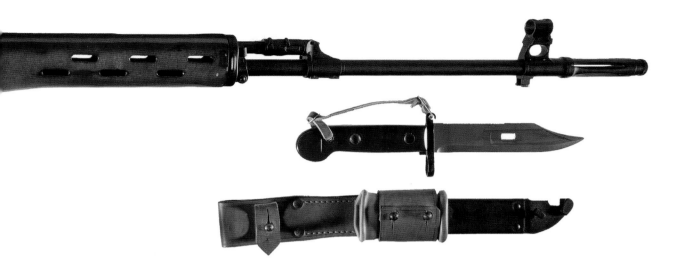

bore brush for removing residues from the bore. A two-ended screwdriver blade had a range of functions, specifically engaging with various screws and clips during the disassembly and reassembly process, cleaning out the gas port and gas tube and altering the elevation of the front sight. A drift punch was used for removing punch-type fittings during disassembly. A combination tool had storage and utility functions. For storage, the body of the tool could be used to store the jag, bore brush, screwdriver blade and drift punch, but it also acted as a handle for many

The official Soviet-issue kit pouches for the SVD, PSO-1 optical sight and magazines. The bag (top right) is the dust cover for the PSO-1 when it was fitted to the SVD but not in use. The sight/ magazine bag had four pouches for magazines, two external and two internal. (Photo courtesy of Rock Island Auction Company)

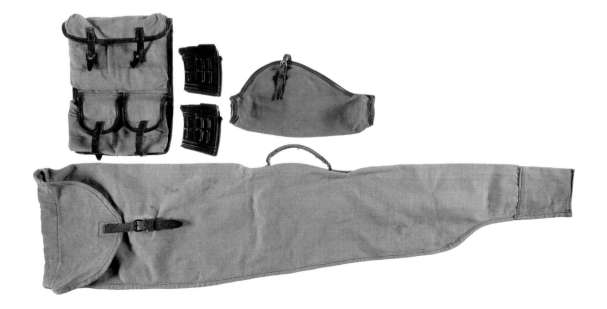

of these same items. When fitted with the screwdriver, for example, the tool could be used for removal of the gas tube and reassembly. Finally, illustrations in the SVD manual show a dual-compartment, dual-cap, Mosin-Nagant rifle-type oiler bottle. One compartment of the bottle would contain a solvent cleaning solution while the other would hold the lubricating oil.

Because the PSO-1 optical sight was integral to the function of the SVD, it also came with a spare parts and maintenance kit. This consisted of ten items: two spare batteries; three spare light bulbs (for reticle illumination); a protective case for holding the light bulbs; a light filter (to be fitted to the ocular lens on the sight to improve visual acuity when there are reduced-visibility conditions); a key-screwdriver tool; a rubber fitting for the toggle switch; and a wad of tissues for wiping down the sight.

The Soviet sniper was supplied with three bags and pouches for the rifle and accessories. The first was a large bag that had internal pockets for the PSO-1, four magazines, and most of the rifle-cleaning and maintenance kit and PSO-1 accessories. There was a separate pouch for the winter reticule illumination apparatus, spare batteries and oiler bottle. The sniper was also provided with a dust cover to slip over the PSO-1 when it was *in situ* on the SVD, for protection of the sensitive optical sight when it was not in use.

MAINTENANCE

Most of the official instruction in the SVD manual follows the generic principles of firearms maintenance, but some more distinctive points are worth highlighting for comment. Notably, the instructions continue to reflect the highly centralized Soviet thinking, the manual stating that the cleaning and oiling of the rifle had to take place under the observant scrutiny of the squad leader and occasionally of an officer. Once the disassembled rifle had been cleaned, the squad leader would inspect the components to his satisfaction and only then would the rifle be approved for use.

Given the Soviet historical experience of fighting in wide extremes of climate, the SVD manual is prescriptive about which types of cleaning, oiling and lubricating solutions could be used within particular temperature spectrums. The 'liquid rifle lubricant' has the broadest utility, suited for general cleaning and lubrication in air temperatures from −50°C to +50°C. The 'rifle lubricant', by contrast, is specified for cleaning and lubricating the bore and moving parts only *after* the weapon has been cleaned. Furthermore, it is only approved for use at temperatures above 5°C. Finally, the 'rifle bore cleaning solution' is a more potent solvent designed for removing hardened propellant fouling from the bore, bolt and other parts of the rifle directly subjected to propellant gases. This cleaning solution has no temperature restrictions, but the neat solution has to be prepared by mixing 1 litre of water with 200g of ammonium carbonate and 3–5g of potassium dichromate.

This Russian soldier on exercise in 2017 has thoroughly winterized his SVD by applying white fabric or paint to most of its surfaces. Properly lubricated, the SVD and the PSO-1 will function down to temperatures of –50°C. (Mil.ru/ Wikimedia/CC BY-SA 4.0)

FIRING THE SVD

Operating the SVD is, in mechanical terms, much like the experience of working with an AK assault rifle. The magazine is filled with cartridges (typically nine, although it will take ten) and inserted into the magazine well until it engages with the magazine latch.

To load the weapon, first the selector switch is pushed one click down into the 'Fire' position; like the AK, this enables the cocking handle to be drawn to the rear and released, allowing the bolt to ride forward, strip a

The SVD is a light sniping rifle, but also a long one, measuring 1,225mm even without the bayonet-knife fitting attached, as evidenced by this photo. Although this Kurdish sniper appears to be taking aim for a shot, the position of the selector lever is on 'Safe'. (Kurdishstruggle/Wikimedia/ CC BY 2.0)

cartridge from the top of the magazine and chamber it. The sniper can then either return the selector switch to its start position, which prevents the rifle from being fired, or take the shot. Being a semi-automatic weapon, the SVD fires a shot with each trigger pull, automatically reloading between the rounds.

If there are stoppages, in most cases misfeeds, misfires, jammed cartridges or failures to eject can be cleared simply by recharging the cocking handle to expel the problematic cartridge or reset the rifle. A failure to extract might require more involved clearance procedures, however, holding the bolt back and open while the cartridge is manually extracted.

When the magazine has emptied its cartridges, the bolt automatically holds open on a bolt-stop. All the sniper now needs to do to continue shooting is to press the magazine latch and release the empty magazine, insert a fresh magazine, draw the bolt to the rear and release once again.

SOVIET SNIPERS AND THE SVD

It is worth clarifying some details about the way in which the SVD was distributed in the Soviet Army of the Cold War era. In the 1980s, the SVD was within the tables of organization and equipment (TO&E) of the motorized rifle squad. Each squad was transported within an armoured personnel carrier (APC) or infantry fighting vehicle (IFV), the mainstays being the BMP, BRDM and BTR families. The squad consisted of nine men in total, split between two or three men operating the vehicle (the number of men doing so varied depending on the type of vehicle), while the remainder acted as dismounted infantry. There were three squads in a motorized rifle platoon, and one man in one of these squads would be equipped with an SVD rifle. The eight remaining personnel of this squad manning a BMP vehicle carried a variety of weapons.

Three members of the squad – the assistant squad leader/BMP gunner, the BMP driver/mechanic and the RPG-armed grenadier – carried the 9mm Makarov pistol as a back-up sidearm, their hands being preoccupied with other weaponry and duties. Four others – the squad leader/BMP commander, the rifleman/medic, the senior rifleman and the rifleman/assistant grenadier – had the standard assault rifle of the day, the 5.45mm AK-74, which began replacing the 7.62mm AK-47/AKM from the late 1970s; the AK-74's effective range was about 400m.

Automatic suppressive fire at squad level came from the squad machine-gunner's 7.62mm RPK-74 light machine gun: this was essentially an AK-74 with a longer and heavier fixed barrel, an integral bipod mount and an extended 45-round magazine. (The standard AK-74 magazine had a 30-round capacity, although the weapon could take the RPK-74 extended magazines.) Opinion on the effective range of the RPK-74 seems mixed. The weapon itself had iron sights calibrated out to 1,000m, but given the absence of optical sights and the limitations of human vision this seems optimistic, certainly against human-sized point targets. In reality, point shooting effective range would have been little different from that

of the AK-74, perhaps squeezing out an extra 100m on account of the stabilization provided by the bipod and the ballistic advantages of the heavier barrel.

This left the SVD, carried by one rifleman, as the primary instrument at both squad and platoon levels for commanding ranges in excess of 500m. Only at company and battalion levels did the TO&E begin to introduce heavier long-range support weapons, such as the 7.62mm PKM machine gun in the motorized rifle platoon's machine-gun company and mortars and automatic grenade launchers at the battalion level. A similar organizational distribution of the SVD was also used in the naval-infantry forces. A naval-infantry company, for example, would have one SVD sniper per three-squad infantry platoon.

Note that in these organizational tiers there are no other sniping weapons designated. The SVD was *the* tool of long-range precision infantry firepower, doctrinally and structurally. The guidance provided by the official SVD manual reveals how the actions of the Soviet SVD sniper were less about the independent, adaptive actions we tend to associate with modern Western snipers, and more about the sniper's integration into the centralized command processes of the Soviet Army. While the manual acknowledges that the sniper can act unilaterally if the situation warrants, it also states that both the firing position chosen and the actual act of firing can be governed by direct orders from the sniper's commander (the squad or platoon leader). The manual details the specific commands the sniper is likely to receive, including: instructions to move to an

In the 1990s, Russian military practice broadly followed the Soviet model. Here, a Russian sniper of the Western Military District conducts winter tactical training with his SVD, using his ski poles as an improvised bipod. His SVD has the plastic furniture that replaced the wood during the 1990s and he also appears to have the rifle fitted with a collapsible buttstock. (Russian Defence Ministry/Handout/Anadolu Agency via Getty Images)

identified firing position; commands to load and prepare to fire; identification of the target; windage and elevation corrections to input into the optical sight; fire and cease-fire commands; and orders to unload the rifle. Such detailed instruction implies, or perhaps hopes, that the commander would himself have significant sniping expertise.

Soviet infantry were typically selected for sniper training during the first week of their two-year conscript military service. During introductory firearms training, the recruits were instructed in marksmanship using the standard-issue AK-47 or AK-74 over ranges of up to 300m. They were evaluated not only on their ability to achieve satisfactory shot groups, but also whether they could hit human-shaped silhouette targets at practical combat distances. If they demonstrated some promise with a firearm during this phase, they might be selected for further evaluation with the SVD. This involved familiarization with the weapon and the PSO-1 scope and the opportunity to put rounds down range, out to about 400m. Should they continue to impress, they would be officially selected for sniper training.

In August 1982, the US Defense Intelligence Agency published a *Review of the Soviet Ground Forces*, which included an article explaining the training of the Cold War Soviet Army sniper. It outlined how the SVD-equipped sniper was trained at three different 'stations':

At station one training begins with a detailed study of the sniper's weapon, the SVD rifle, and its telescopic sight. The basic elements of rifle firing are studied in depth, including principles of trajectory and accuracy, and the effects of weather and ballistics on the round. Firing is done in pairs, while in various postures. Students are also required to change firing positions while observing the principles of cover and concealment.

At station two the soldiers are taught to estimate the speed and direction of moving targets and to fire on them in various ways. They are taught to use the fine adjustments on the sight and to lead a moving target. The soldiers are also taught the rules of adjusting a sight for a sidewind.

At station three training concentrates on observing targets, selecting appropriate range scales and reticles, estimating distances and making the necessary sight adjustment.

The author makes the interesting observation that new sniper trainees, who have been carefully selected from among the unit's best marksmen, initially do poorly with the SVD because they are not accustomed to using telescopic sights. (Defense Intelligence Agency 1982: 17–18)

The point about the new SVD-equipped snipers struggling with the PSO-1 scope is perhaps not as significant as the author argues. A first encounter with firearms optics can be an awkward process of adjustment, as the shooter attempts to chase down a good reticle picture that bobs, weaves and disappears while he is attempting to find the correct eye relief and a consistent cheek weld to the stock in relation to the sight.

The article's reference to learning firing positions chimes with a dedicated chapter in the official SVD manual. The manual explains how the soldier should move into position with the rifle, particularly when crawling – he is advised to crawl forward with the left side of his body pressed to the ground, pushing with his right leg while keeping his left leg crooked as a platform for the receiver of the SVD, keeping the operating parts clear of the ground. Meanwhile, his right arm holds the muzzle of the SVD off the ground by means of the sling swivel, while his left arm assists the push forward.

Regarding actual firing positions, the following were taught for the SVD: prone; kneeling; sitting (with heels on the ground, legs open or in a cross-legged position); and standing. There were also detailed instructions for firing the rifle from a front rest or from behind vertical cover such as a tree or the side of a wall. Notably, in prone position shooting and for firing at aerial targets (see below), the manual gives the option of positioning the front hand either on the forend or wrapped around the front of the magazine. Holding the magazine of a firearm is not usually a recommended practice, as it can affect feeding and result in more 'muzzle flip', degrading follow-up shots. There is also a safety concern – if the rifle has a serious malfunction and the receiver explodes, the shooter gripping the magazine or magazine well might lose a few fingers. The illustrations that accompany this practice in the manual suggests that holding the magazine has utility if the shooter is using a front rest, the placement of which precludes placing the hand on the forend, or when shooting at high-angle targets such as aircraft, when moving the hand as close to the receiver as possible assists in achieving a high angle of elevation.

Russian soldiers man a checkpoint near a military hospital in Dushanbe, Tajikistan, in 2001. The young soldier on the left has an SVD at the ready, and would receive firing and tactical instructions from the senior lieutenant in the middle. (Wojtek Laski/Getty Images)

SERVICE AND COMBAT DEBUT

Details about the specific numbers of SVDs produced from 1963 appear impossible to pin down with any precision. Firearms expert Max Popenker, in his informative exposition of SVD history for the Forgotten Weapons YouTube channel, explains that while the Izhmash factory was producing about 500,000 AK assault rifles every year during the 1970s, annual SVD units numbered about 5,000–7,000, perhaps occasionally reaching above the 10,000 mark (Forgotten Weapons 2019). Although the comparison between the AK and the SVD can make the SVD numbers appear like limited issue, in fact these are high volumes for a sniping rifle. Not only did Izhmash have to satisfy orders from within the Soviet Union, but also those from other members of the Eastern Bloc and communist allies, including Albania, Bulgaria, Czechoslovakia, East Germany and Hungary, as they switched to the SVD. In Czechoslovakia, for example, the principal sniping instrument of the first decades of the Cold War was the 7.62mm vz.54, a bolt-action weapon with a Mosin-Nagant action, a free-floating barrel, a stock with improved sniper ergonomics and fitted with a 2.5× Meopta scope. During the 1970s, however, the vz.54 was replaced by the SVD.

Details about the SVD's very first forays into combat are scant. Likely the very first instance of SVD combat sniping occurred during the Vietnam War (1963–75). At some point during the 1970s, SVDs apparently crept into the arsenals of the People's Army of Vietnam (PAVN) in very small numbers, as part of the general flow of material aid from the Soviet Union to communist North Vietnam from the mid-1960s. The SVD was an expensive rarity for the North Vietnamese soldiers, however, so much so that some sources claim US intelligence agencies were offering a $25,000 reward for every weapon captured – clearly the SVD was either making an impression tactically or the US authorities were simply eager to conduct their own analysis of a weapon at the forefront of small-arms innovation. Forum posts by US veterans of the Vietnam War remark on seeing captured SVDs, either in Vietnam itself or in arsenals or ordnance test facilities stateside. There are only a small number of photographs showing SVDs actually in the hands of PAVN soldiers, and the author has not

found any information explaining how the SVD fitted into PAVN training, TO&Es and tactics. Likely the SVD was simply swapped out for the Mosin-Nagant-type rifles that were the more common PAVN sniping weapon.

As we have seen, the later Chinese incursion into Vietnam in 1979 led to the capture of Soviet SVDs, from which the Chinese reverse-engineered the 7.62mm Type 79, later the 7.62mm Type 85. This weapon also went into combat in the 1980s, in the sporadic series of border clashes between China and Vietnam that punctuated the decade. Although historical details about sniper deployment and operations during this conflict are limited, one interesting issue to emerge is that regarding ammunition. According to some researchers, while the Chinese now had their own semi-automatic sniping rifle, what they did not have were supplies of precision ammunition such as the Soviet 7N1. Instead they used regular 7.62×54mmR ball ammunition, as fed into Mosin-Nagant rifles and Soviet machine guns, in the Type 79/85, with a predictable diminution of accuracy compared to the more carefully crafted sniping cartridges. Poor relations between the Soviet Union and China at this time meant that the Chinese could not acquire stocks of the precision ammunition on the market (the fractious relations were one of the main reasons why China developed an unlicensed SVD copy in the first place). Given the situation, we might expect the Chinese to have developed their own sniping ammunition, but this does not appear to have been the case, and Chinese snipers simply soldiered on with the standard ball rounds, adapting their scope set-up, range expectations and shooting style accordingly.

Although to modern eyes this might appear as the most slapdash approach to solving the problem, Chinese snipers would still be able to get reasonably effective service out of the Type 79/85, in the same way that Mosin-Nagant-equipped snipers firing standard ammunition during World War II were a lethal threat to Axis forces. During the Sino-Vietnamese border clashes, furthermore, the ranges of engagement were often relatively short at about 200–400m, so a sniper familiar with the characteristics of his rifle and of the ammunition, however basic the latter was, would still be able to extract usable performance over these ranges.

The rifle shown here is a piece of history, being one of the few SVD-63s captured from People's Army of Vietnam (PAVN) forces during the Vietnam War. The documentation registering the weapon as a 'War Trophy' indicates that the date of capture, or at least registration, was 19 December 1974. Markings on the weapon indicate that it was produced in 1972. The trigger housing is marked 'CHE TAO TAI LIEN-XO' on the left side, a North Vietnamese designation for equipment supplied by the Soviet Union. (Photos courtesy of Rock Island Auction Company)

THE SVD IN AFGHANISTAN

Afghanistan was in many ways the true proving ground of the SVD. The Soviet–Afghan War (1979–89) was not only the Soviet Union's first major international conflict since the end of World War II, it was also one in which the sniper could excel. The initial Soviet occupation of Afghanistan devolved into a decade-long counter-insurgency war, fought with exceptional brutality across a vast and unforgiving landscape.

As Western Coalition forces discovered from 2001, Afghanistan is a country of wide plains, deep valleys and towering mountains, with plentiful features – riverbeds, irrigation ditches, patches of bush or woodland, concentrations of thick-walled rural housing, rocky clefts and outcrops, mountainous crags – for movement behind as cover and concealment. In these environments, medium- to long-range observation and precision fire could be the decisive factor in the outcome of an engagement. The Soviet forces soon discovered that SVD-armed soldiers had a critical tactical role to play combating Mujahideen combatants who moved fluidly around a landscape they knew intimately, and blended quickly into it when attacked.

The increasingly challenging tactical conditions of Afghanistan led to a reorganization of the distribution of Soviet SVD snipers among the infantry platoons. Instead of one SVD sniper per three-squad platoon, every squad would have its own sniper, tripling the long-range firepower of the platoon. The SVD was also used heavily by Soviet Spetsnaz special forces, who specialized in long-range airborne insertion operations deep into enemy territory. A core mission of Spetsnaz units was the interdiction of Mujahideen supply convoys in remote parts of the country, especially in the east as the convoys passed from depots in Pakistan through the eastern tribal mountainous regions into the Afghan hinterland.

One of the most revealing insights into the operational use of the SVD comes from an article by Marco Vorobiev, a former Spetznaz soldier and Soviet–Afghan War veteran. He describes the SVD through the prism of one particular operation, a mission to ambush and destroy a large Mujahideen convoy travelling through a remote part of Afghanistan. A significant part of the article is devoted to explaining his training in and orientation to the SVD, however, thus providing a first-hand user insight into the weapon from a special-forces perspective.

Vorobiev had been drafted into the VDV airborne forces in 1985, attending the training centre in Fergana, Uzbekistan. He recounts how he quickly fell in love with both the SVD and sniper shooting. The initial challenge was actually to find the reticle of the PSO-1 sight, a problem eventually solved through a correct understanding of eye relief. Once he could see and understand the reticle, which he found 'ingenious', he noted that he was quickly knocking down targets with ease at 200–400m.

Following his introduction to the rifle, Vorobiev embarked on three months of sniper training. Beyond gaining an intimate functional understanding of the SVD and the PSO-1, this training included elements such as memorizing ballistic tables, tactics for engaging multiple targets, field craft in mountainous terrain and conducting long-range reconnaissance. At the end of the training, Vorobiev was assigned to a Spetznaz platoon and sent to Afghanistan, a place that, as an active war zone, would be a live theatre for cementing his new-found sniper skills.

Vorobiev notes that the primary role of the Soviet sniper in Afghanistan was to take out high-value targets and heavy-weapons teams and provide overwatch during assaults and ambushes. The SVD was ideal for counteracting Mujahideen 'shoot and run' tactics, the rifle being able to reach the attackers as they made their retreat across the other side of a river or ravine following an attack. Vorobiev also explains how the SVD snipers would use B-32 armour-piercing/incendiary bullets to penetrate Mujahideen fortified positions and to stop moving vehicles. An interesting contextual point comes from Vorobiev's recollections about the SVD's range capabilities, taking us back to our opening debate on the SVD as sniping rifle or a DMR. When acting in support of ambushes or assaults,

A Soviet infantry platoon mount up in their BMP-1 infantry fighting vehicles during operations in Afghanistan. Although the blurred nature of this photograph obscures the precise identification of weaponry, at least one of these individuals would be equipped with an SVD. (NARA)

Vorobiev explains that the SVD was most accurate and consistent out to about 400m. If the sniper was using light ball ammunition, it worked 'well enough', although only if 'tight grouping was not very important' (Vorobiev 2011). The PSO-1 scope also excelled in the 0–400m range, Vorobiev noting that it not only provided a wide field of view for quick target acquisition, but also allowed the sniper to shift across this range spectrum quickly without having to adjust the scope turrets.

Apparently, the SVD had a certain celebrity attached to it in the minds of non-snipers in Afghanistan. Vorobiev describes APC crews swarming around him and his rifle prior to departure on the mission, the regular troops wanting to hold the weapon and have their picture taken with it, eager to send the snap home. While aesthetics come well down the list of a sniping rifle's core requirements, the SVD certainly looks purposeful and powerful, and evidently exerted a martial attraction upon those around it.

Returning to Vorobiev's combat mission in Afghanistan, the Spetsnaz forces deployed to conduct the ambush numbered 67 men. They were very heavily armed, their weapons including RPG-7 and RPG-18 anti-tank rocket grenade launchers, 12.7mm NSV heavy machine guns and AGS-17 belt-fed grenade launchers. Vorobiev was the only SVD sniper among the group, although he does note that there were two AKMS assault rifles fitted with suppressors.

The mission began with an airlift by Mi-8MT transport helicopters, which took the troops to an insertion point some 10km from the intended engagement area, the Spetsnaz personnel then hiking the distance with onerous individual kit loads of 35–40kg. Once at their location, the team prepared the site for the ambush, setting up anti-tank and anti-personnel mines and fire sectors for the various weapons. Vorobiev's position was on high ground about 150m from the 'kill zone', a position that provided

Afghanistan, 1985 (opposite)

A Soviet Spetsnaz sniper dressed in KLMK camouflaged overalls takes aim at a Mujahideen target with his PSO-1-equipped SVD from a scrubby position in mountainous terrain. It is the summer months, thus the green vegetation around him provides concealment, while a rocky outcrop provides cover and a stabilizing front rest. He is wearing an SVD ammunition pouch on his right hip and has an RD-54 backpack placed on the ground beside him, hidden behind the front cover but within arm's reach, containing extra mission tools. The target is a Mujahideen soldier. In this case the enemy is evidently at very close range, and the SVD's semi-automatic functionality will prove useful, giving the sniper the means to move his point of aim (POA) onto a second Mujahideen warrior rapidly, without the delay imposed by the operation of a bolt action. At the opposite extreme of such short-range shooting, the Soviet–Afghan War also produced examples of long-range accuracy with the SVD. According to several sources, one Sergeant Vladimir Ilyin shot and killed a Mujahideen commander at a range of 1,350m in the Panjshir Gorge during the 1980s. Details of this event are sketchy, and the range of the shot is certainly at the absolute limit of the SVD and its cartridge. Whether it was a matter of luck or judgement, such a shot would have been a challenge for even the most highly developed sniping rifles and expert snipers.

him with an excellent visual overview of the site, both laterally and in depth. He and many of the other team members also constructed 'shooting protective structures' using rocks and boulders, these offering both cover and concealment. Vorobiev was located next to one Sergeant Efimenko, a PKM machine-gunner. The two weapons fired essentially the same cartridge over the same effective range, but while the PKM could lay down belts of full-auto suppressive fire against area targets, the SVD was better attuned to zeroing in on individual personnel. Now all that was required was to wait and spring the ambush.

Vorobiev's account of the early moments of the action paint a devastating picture of firepower unleashed against the men, animals and vehicles of the Mujahideen supply column when it moved into their sights. Vorobiev recounts near-effortless kills, the PSO-1 sight enabling him to snap quickly between targets while Efimenko's machine gun drove the Mujahideen to the ground with suppressive fire. Vorobiev had already pre-ranged the kill zone before the firefight, but in those cases in which the range was unknown the rangefinder and the hold-off chevrons of the PSO-1 sight enabled him to adjust to fresh targets almost instantly. He also praises the SVD's semi-automatic function, which allowed him to move his POA without disruption and increased the rapidity of the kills.

The first 15 minutes of the ambush inflicted a high number of kills upon the supply convoy. Many of the surviving Mujahideen in Vorobiev's sector went to ground, attempting to shield themselves from fire behind heavy cover. The extensive trailing length of the convoy meant that the small Spetsnaz unit had only been able to trap a portion of it within the kill zone, however, and the aggressively minded and tactically astute Mujahideen outside the kill zone therefore began to mount a counter-attack against the Soviet ambush positions on the left flank. Many of the assault troops around Vorobiev now moved to support the left flank against the emerging threat, but Vorobiev and his fire-support group, located about 350–400m from the left-flank battle, stayed in place to provide security on the right flank and overwatch across a predesignated extraction route. Nevertheless, he was still able to contribute to the battle at range, explaining that he raised the setting on his BDC and started to engage long-range targets.

Rather than shooting at any Mujahideen who presented himself, Vorobiev's main concern now was to target enemy vehicles deploying heavy weaponry. He soon spotted one: a flat-bed truck with a 12.7mm DShK heavy machine gun mounted on the rear and carrying about five or six Mujahideen combatants plus a 'Dushka' machine-gunner. At a distance of about 800m, most of the Mujahideen soldiers dismounted, leaving the truck manned by the driver and the machine-gunner. Vorobiev placed the third chevron of the PSO-1 sight onto the driver-side windscreen, to allow for the bullet drop at the extended range, and took the shot. He felt he observed the impact on the front bumper of the now-moving vehicle, so adjusted his POA and fired another round, this time killing the driver. The truck swerved to the side of the road and hit bordering rocks. The machine-gunner, momentarily unsettled, climbed behind the DShK and prepared to open fire, but with the shot elevation now calculated,

Soviet soldiers of the 56th Separate Air Assault Brigade conduct a combat mission in the Wardak province of Afghanistan during the Soviet–Afghan War. Although these troops do not have an SVD on display, snipers were often deployed to provide protective overwatch to patrols like this. Most of these infantry are armed with the 5.45mm AKS-74, a folding-stock airborne forces version of the standard AK-74. The man nearest the camera carries an RPO-A Shmel disposable rocket launcher. (E. Kuvakin/Wikimedia/ CC BY-SA 3.0)

Vorobiev dropped him with his next round. The convoy ambush battle culminated in the arrival of a ground-attack mission by two squadrons of Su-25 ground-attack aircraft, then helicopter extraction for the Spetsnaz team.

In this narrative, we find a perfect demonstration of the rationale behind the SVD. The convoy ambush provided a target-rich environment requiring engagement at speed across a broad expanse of territory. Vorobiev's SVD excelled under these tactical conditions. The rifle's semi-automatic function meant that he could add to the overall weight of fire needed to gain fire superiority, but with sharp target selection and precise accuracy. He also engaged targets across a range spectrum of about 300–800m, showing how the optimal range of about 400m could easily be exceeded if the situation warranted. Vorobiev singled out the PSO-1 scope for particular praise on account of its ease of use.

The war in Afghanistan also saw the Soviets optimize SVD snipers in some truly distinctive ways. In a RAND Corporation report prepared for the US Army in May 1998, the author Alexander Alexiev was told by a former soldier in the Soviet Army's air-assault brigades that on one operation, six SVD-armed snipers were placed aboard a Mi-24 gunship helicopter and flown to a position hovering directly above a Mujahideen transport caravan. The snipers engaged the caravan and its occupants simultaneously from the hovering helicopter, killing the insurgents one by one (Alexiev 1988: 30). The SVD would have been perfect for this role, the semi-automatic platform meaning that the snipers would not have had to deal with the awkward action of operating a rifle bolt from the unstable and shifting helicopter.

Afghanistan was an informative 'classroom' for the Soviets when it came to sniper employment. If used with appropriate tactics, especially in ambushes or to provide medium-range support during infantry battles, the SVD could make a vital contribution to the outcome of an engagement. There were other lessons learned, however. The SVD, unlike the AK assault rifles, was more vulnerable to malfunctions through exposure to battlefield dirt and hard use, so regular and diligent cleaning was a necessity. Also, Soviet snipers found the SVD's lack of integral bipod an issue, especially when they were compelled to move positions frequently and achieve rifle stabilization at each firing point purely through either hold technique or an improvised front rest. In response, many of the Soviet snipers in Afghanistan fitted their SVDs with bipods taken from RPK light machine guns (Grau & Cutshaw 2002: 9).

ACCURACY AND THE PSO-1 SCOPE

Vorobiev's enthusiasm for the PSO-1 warrants some further investigation as to why it is such a practical combat scope, particularly the way in which the sight's reticle design facilitates fast elevation and windage calculations. The SVD's semi-automatic capability thrives on the advantages set by this sight arrangement.

The bottom-left portion of the PSO-1 sight's reticle consists of a stadiametric range-estimation instrument, based on the average height of a human male at 1.7m. To estimate the distance to the human target, the sniper places the feet of the enemy soldier on the solid horizontal base line and then moves the sight laterally until the head of the target just touches the sloping segmented range line. The numbers of this segmented line indicate the range in hundreds of metres. So, for example, if the enemy soldier's feet touch the baseline and his head touches the arcing line half-way between the '2' and the '4' on the scale, this indicates that he is roughly 300m away from the shooter. The system is rapid and effective, but comes with the caveat that it can only be used with reassurance if the full height of the target figure is visible. In other cases, the sniper has to calculate range using one of several alternative methods, including visual estimations from known features or by applying mil formulae.

Once the sniper has defined the range to the target, he uses the PSO-1 to calculate and apply the correct elevation to the shot. He can do this by adjusting the elevation drum, but the PSO-1 includes a more rapid system. The main aiming point on the PSO-1 sight's reticle is the uppermost of four vertically arranged chevrons. These provide rapid elevation calculations without the requirement to alter the elevation drum, the elevation accorded to each chevron differing according to the distance at which the rifle is zeroed to the top chevron. Taking a typical zeroing point of 100m, chevron no. 1 (the uppermost of the four chevrons) is used for ranges of 100–400m, chevron no. 2 (working from the top down) is used for ranges around 500–600m, chevron no. 3 is for 600–700m and chevron no. 4 is 800–1000m. The chevrons can also be used to extend the maximum range of the SVD beyond a zeroed point of 1,000m – each of

the three chevrons below the uppermost one adds 100m to the range, taking it up to 1,300m.

With practice, the Dragunov-equipped sniper can apply the fine grades of the reticle to adjust fire across ranges very quickly. For example, if the rifle is zeroed to 100m, at ranges of 100–200m the sniper will simply place the tip of the upper chevron dead centre on the chest of a human target. At 300m, however, he can place the same chevron tip on the face of the target, which has the effect of giving the bullet some allowance for drop into the chest area. At 400m, the sniper instead hovers the baseline of the upper chevron on top of the target's head like a visual hat, the bottom of the 'legs' of the chevron either side of the top of the skull. Pulling the trigger will again, all other things being well, put the shot in the same place as the preceding three shots (i.e. centre chest). For a 500m shot, the sniper puts the tip of the second chevron on the target's beltline or navel, again to deliver a chest shot, this time by allowing for a little rise in relation to the chevron point. And so on it goes, the sniper progressively learning the hold-over points of each chevron until he can achieve the correct aim point with little conscious calculation.

The fluid use of ranging scale and elevation chevrons on the PSO-1 is integral to the SVD's combat performance. The system is both intuitive to understand and quick to use in practised hands, as we saw in Vorobiev's battle experience in Afghanistan. Extending out from the uppermost chevron there is also a windage correction scale, bordered on each side by the number '10'. As with the four vertically arranged chevrons, the windage scale is to be used in combat situations that are moving too fast to allow for the methodical adjustment of the windage dial on the scope body. The scale is marked out in mils, and the sniper's training and experience will lead him to apply the correct hold-off point. For example, if the sniper is shooting at a target about 500m away in a heavy crosswind, he might place the target in line with the 5-mil point on the windward side of the target.

The sniper can also use the windage scale to apply lead to a moving target. The official SVD manual provides a table to explain how this is done at common distances and against typical moving targets. For example, when firing against a human target at a distance of 200m, running directly across the sniper's field of view, the sniper needs to apply 0.8m of lead to allow the bullet to intersect with the target at the POA. He can either do this by aiming an estimated 1.5 extra body widths ahead of the target or he can place the running figure at the 4-mil point on the windage reticle, on the side at which the figure is running towards the central post of the scale. Similarly, if the sniper is shooting at a vehicle moving at 20km/h at a distance of 800m, placing the vehicle at the 10-mil point on the scale will give the correct lead.

Another recommended way given to calculate windage with the SVD is to adjust the rifle based on visual impacts in relation to the windage scale, much like the fire adjustment process of traditional artillery fire. So if the first shot against a target is observed to land 3 mils to the left of the central chevron, then the sniper can simply place the target on the 3-mil point of impact on the scale for the follow-up shot. Again, the semi-automatic platform of the SVD means that the sniper can do this very quickly.

One particularly interesting table presented at the back of the SVD manual provides figures on the quantity of ammunition required for a sniper to defeat a single type of target at ranges of 100–300m. The targets listed are: head shot; television camera; head and shoulders; head to waist; running figure (in profile); running figure; machine gun; anti-tank missile; anti-tank gun. So, for example, at ranges of 100–300m, the manual's authors allow for just one round to achieve a head-shot kill, but this creeps up to two shots at 400m, three at 500m, four at 600m, six at 700m and eight at 800m (by which time we might surmise that the target would know he was being shot at and would have found some cover). To defeat/destroy a machine gun, from 100–500m a single shot is required, creeping up to two for 600–800m, three for 900m, four for 1,000m, six for 1,100m, nine for 1,200m, and an implausible and ammunition-consuming 12 shots for 1,300m. Strangely, at 1,300m only five shots are required to defeat an anti-tank missile and three shots for an anti-tank gun; perhaps the heavy fire required for a machine gun indicates the presence of the multiple members of the machine-gun team and the smaller size of the target in comparison to the other weapon systems, but it does leave many questions begging.

The SVD manual also gives instructions for taking shots at aircraft and helicopters. Engaging aerial targets with a single-shot or semi-automatic rifle is certainly ambitious, and often impractical due to the range, speed, altitude and offensive capabilities of fixed-wing or rotary-wing military aircraft. Furthermore, even firing an armour-piercing bullet it is extremely unlikely that the sniper will inflict sufficient damage with one or two hits to bring the aircraft down. This being said, sniping rifles do have utility against helicopters in a low hover or making a low-and-slow pass, the best target point being the pilot rather than the helicopter itself, although engine compartments and tail-rotor blades are also vulnerable to sniper shots. There have been numerous instances of Coalition helicopters being struck by SVD sniper fire in Iraq and Afghanistan, and while the impacts are usually not sufficient enough to destroy the helicopter, they can certainly compel the pilot to exit the area quickly and change or abandon the mission.

The SVD manual's guidance on engaging aerial targets is quite detailed. The firing positions demonstrated are supine (lying on the back, not the front), kneeling, standing and from a trench position. In each case the illustration shows the shooter gripping the SVD by the magazine, not the forend, with his left hand, making the required muzzle elevation easier to achieve. Recognizing the limitations of individual fire, the authors advise the sniper that engaging aircraft is only to be conducted alongside additional fire from other members of the squad or platoon; only when engaging parachutists should the sniper fire independently. The manual recommends using armour-piercing incendiary bullets against aircraft if they are available, and conventional ball and tracer ammunition if they are not.

The most complex element about firing on aircraft is lead calculation, made more fiendish by the fact that an astute pilot will typically be adjusting the angle of flight continually. When firing at an aircraft diving towards the sniper, the manual advises him to set the rear sight at '4' or 'П' (a constant sight setting that corresponds with '4') and aim at the front of the target, opening fire at a range of 700–900m. Interestingly, when engaging helicopters specifically, the manual instructs the sniper to use the

scope at ranges of up to 300m and iron sights at ranges greater than 300m, likely because the sniper's peripheral vision outside the iron sights will give a wider field of view at the longer ranges, and make lead adjustment easier. Engaging helicopters flying at speeds below 150m/sec involves the 'tracking method' of fire, the sniper calculating the magnitude of lead either through metres or multiplications of fuselage length (a calculation table is provided in the manual) and maintaining that distance throughout the sequence of fire. For aircraft travelling faster than 150m/sec, the manual instead recommends

A Russian sniper takes aim at Chechen fighters from a position in the village of Sergen-Yurt, south-east of Grozny, 25 January 2000. The trigger guard of the SVD is widened sufficiently for snipers to be able to operate the rifle while wearing gloves. (AFP via Getty Images)

the 'barrier method', in which the sniper fires repeated shots at a fixed point on the aircraft's flightpath, continuing firing until the aircraft has flown through that point and hopefully is struck as it does so.

Although it is fiendishly difficult to engage aircraft with a sniping rifle, there are historical examples of SVD aerial kills. One of the most impressive occurred on 12 November 1989 near San Miguel in El Salvador. A sniper from the left-wing insurgent group Farabundo Martí National Liberation Front engaged an attacking Salvadoran Air Force Cessna A-37B Dragonfly light ground-attack aircraft with his SVD, aiming for the cockpit. A round struck and incapacitated the pilot and the aircraft plunged into the ground. There are also some claims that Iraqi insurgents downed US RQ-11 Raven hand-launched remote-controlled unmanned aerial vehicles in Iraq.

THE SVD IN THE WIDER WORLD

Even as the Soviet forces were labouring their way to defeat in Afghanistan, the SVD was making its presence felt on international battlefields further afield. This was particularly the case in the Middle East, a region into which the Soviets poured arms and military aid to bolster communist-aligned regimes and insurgencies. Large numbers of Russian-produced SVDs, plus indigenous copies made by Iran and Iraq, meant that the SVD became the sniper tool of choice in many of the region's struggles, including various conflicts in the Lebanon between 1975 and 2000 and the epic war between Iran and Iraq in 1980–88, in which both sides utilized SVDs or SVD-type rifles.

The Iran–Iraq War was, at least until Russia's invasion of Ukraine in 2022, regarded by many as potentially the last conventional war, one in which mass armies clashed in set-piece land battles. It was overwhelmingly an infantry conflict, with huge numbers of often ill-trained soldiers making massed attacks over terrain ideal for snipers in fixed defensive positions – open desert and scrubland, with little in the way of cover or concealment. In this combat environment, it was possible for a talented SVD operator to rack up high tallies of kills in a matter of minutes or hours. The challenge would be to maintain the accuracy of the rifle as it heated up through both firing and the environmental conditions, and having enough ammunition available to engage the targets continually presenting themselves.

The Iran–Iraq War may have spawned the most successful sniper in history, Abdorrasul Zarrin, whose reputation comes despite the fact that he is almost unknown in Western popular history. Zarrin was Iranian, and his number of kills during the Iran–Iraq War is reputedly somewhere between 700 and 3,000. The vagueness of this kill count testifies to the limitations of the sources and inevitable mythologizing. Furthermore, Zarrin did not survive to confirm the exact number (assuming that he could if he was asked), being killed in action in February or March 1984. His story was told in a 2021 Iranian film simply titled *Sniper*, directed by Ali Ghaffari. The few available photographs of Zarrin show him armed

with an SVD, and it is remarkable that of all the sniping rifles in history, it might be the SVD that holds the grim crown for the most kills in the hands of an individual sniper. While Zarrin's kill count may well be exaggerated, the nature of both his weapon and the conflict in which he fought at least provide a basis of plausibility for his position in the sniper league tables.

THE SVD IN CHECHNYA

The searing experience of combat in Afghanistan educated the Soviet military about the importance and tactical impact of SVD-equipped snipers – but further and harder lessons would be learned in another war that erupted shortly after the Soviet withdrawal from Afghanistan in 1989. Following the dissolution of the Soviet Union in 1991, the Russian military left Chechnya, a former Soviet republic, in 1992; but in the logistical chaos of withdrawal they left behind 533 SVD rifles (Grau & Cutshaw 2002: 9), weapons that would ultimately be turned back upon the Russians during the unutterably brutal First Chechen War of 1994–96 and Second Chechen War of 1999–2009.

Lester Grau and Charles Cutshaw have produced one of the most detailed analyses of Russia's sniper war in Chechnya during the 1990s. At the beginning of the conflict in 1994, the Russian Army's ability to deploy well-trained snipers had been degraded. SVD-armed snipers were still present in mechanized infantry units, but general standards of investment and training in the Russian military were woeful in the chaos that followed the break-up of the Soviet Union. Other, more highly trained snipers came from special-operations units within the Ministry of Internal Affairs and Federal Security Service (FSB), but Grau and Cutshaw point out that most of these were trained for law-enforcement and counter-terrorism SWAT (Special Weapons and Tactics)-type raids, and not in the field craft required for open-warfare military sniping. Thus, when deployed to

Chechnya in 1994, Russian sniper teams were not best prepared for what they were about to face, especially in the battle of attrition in the Chechen capital, Grozny. The Chechen fighters, however, had integrated SVD snipers into highly effective combat teams, as Grau and Cutshaw explain:

> Some of the Chechens and their allies who were armed with SVDs deployed as actual snipers, while others joined three- or four-man fighting cells consisting of an RPG gunner, a machinegunner and an SVD marksman, and perhaps an ammunition bearer armed with a Kalashnikov assault rifle. These cells were quite effective as antiarmor hunter-killer teams. The SVD and machinegun fire would pin down supporting infantry while the RPG would engage the armored vehicle. Often four or five cells would work together against a single armored vehicle. Once the fighting moved beyond the cities and into the mountains, Chechen snipers attempted to engage Russian forces at long distances—900 to 1,000 meters away, although terrain and vegetation often limited their engagement ranges. Away from the cities, a Chechen sniper usually operated as part of a team—the sniper plus a four-man support element armed with Kalashnikov assault rifles. The support element usually positioned itself some 500 meters behind the sniper. The sniper would fire one or two shots at the Russians and then change firing positions. Should the Russians fire at the sniper, the support element would open fire at random to draw fire on itself and allow the sniper to escape. (Grau & Cutshaw 2002: 9)

What is striking here is the flexibility of the SVD, its tactical role shifting according to team composition and purpose across a wide range of mission types. Furthermore, Grau and Cutshaw's research indicates that the SVD was being used across nearly its full range spectrum, from

This unit of Chechen fighters in 1995 is likely a tank-killing team. The SVD sniper and the PK machine-gunner would inflict attrition and suppression on supporting infantry, allowing the RPG operator to make a shot on the Russian armour. (Peter Turnley/Corbis/VCG via Getty Images)

relatively close-quarters anti-armour work (the maximum effective range of an RPG-7 is about 330m, so the sniper would be working at close to or slightly beyond that limit) up to shots at 1,000m, even if they were largely for the purposes of suppression.

The First Chechen War was a ghastly experience for the Russian Army, which sustained incessant casualties at the hands of snipers, although they more than gave back death and destruction. Both Russian and Chechen snipers would often shoot enemy soldiers or civilians to wound, drawing out further targets via the subsequent efforts to rescue the wounded person. Chechen snipers would also act as bait to draw Russian counter-sniper missions into merciless ambushes. The presence of a Chechen sniper could bring an entire Russian column to a halt, and the indiscriminate bombardments used against snipers might destroy half a city block in the process. Defence analyst Timothy L. Thomas notes that snipers were used with such intensity that some veterans even refer to the entire conflict as a 'sniper war' (Thomas 2005: 746).

The Russians, however, were taking note. They went into the second half of the 1990s with a better understanding of the tactical impact and unit integration of snipers, and to a large degree imitated the practices of their Chechen enemies. Snipers became increasingly professionalized, aided by the Russian Army's establishment of a modern sniper school in 1999, which implanted stronger field craft and technical skills, reinforced with relevant exercises in Chechnya. All-Army shooting competitions inspiring long-range rifle shooting. The Russians also developed similar hunter-killer detachments to those of the Chechens, consisting of small units of two–four

A group of Chechen fighters in 1996 ready their weapons for combat, the buses behind them containing Russian hostages. The man in the foreground has an SVD; other visible weapons include the AK-74 assault rifle, several RPG-7 anti-tank rocket grenade launchers and RPD light machine guns. (OLEG NIKISHIN/ AFP via Getty Images)

men that included an SVD sniper alongside those armed with RPG-7s, machine guns and/or assault rifles. Two-man sniper teams – both men armed with SVDs – operating with five-man assault teams at distance created effective lure and ambush tactics. Grau and Cutshaw also observed that the elite MVD and FSB snipers received advanced training at the Special Police Detachment facilities near Moscow (Grau & Cutshaw 2002: 10).

Russia's new generation of snipers were back in Chechnya from 1999. The SVD remained the primary weapon, the elite snipers from the security units often fitting their weapons with suppressors to obscure the sniper's firing position. Snipers would exercise more dedication in their combat roles during the Second Chechen War, hiding out in positions for several days and targeting high-value targets that had direct impact on enemy command-and-control. Grau and Cutshaw make further notes of tactics and kit observed in Chechnya in the early 2000s:

> The professional snipers in Chechnya work on the principle of killing the most dangerous enemy first. This is usually an enemy sniper or RPO-A flame-thrower gunner. RPG-7 gunners and machinegunners are usually next, followed by riflemen. A professional sniper is usually equipped with a camouflage (ghillie) suit, a scoped sniper rifle, a machine pistol, binoculars, a radio, a multifunctional knife, an entrenching tool, a load-carrying combat vest, and a backpack. A laser range finder and a periscope are also recommended. (Grau & Cutshaw 2002: 10)

Grau and Cutshaw paint a picture of the SVD-armed sniper not merely operating as a DM in squad support, but as a sniper in the fullest sense.

A Chechen fighter cradles his SVD during a break in the fighting in Chechnya in 1999. During the Second Chechen War (1999–2009), Russian forces employed snipers in far more effective hunter-killer teams, a tactic they had learned partly from Chechen fighters during the First Chechen War (1994–96). (Antoine GYORI/Sygma via Getty Images)

A Russian sniper in Grozny in November 2000 scans the battered landscape for targets using his PSO-1 scope. Note that he has the customary ammunition and optic bag suspended from his belt over his right hip. (Scott Peterson/Liaison via Getty Images)

Carrying a 'machine pistol' (a submachine gun or a shortened assault rifle such as a 5.45mm AKS-74U) suggests that the sniper is working in more solitary fashion, the select-fire weapon there as back-up should he get into a close-quarters tussle with the enemy. The men operating in this way would likely express significant objections to any claim that they are not true snipers, purely on account of their SVD rifle.

While the Russian military did not have an easy ride in the Second Chechen War, it was considerably more effective and professional than the army of the previous conflict, and its snipers played a key role in its subsequent victory in 2009. Andrei Mashukov, a Chechnya veteran, told journalist Alexander Korolkov that during his time in Chechnya he never heard anyone criticize the SVD and observed that a marksman could 'easily' take out an enemy soldier 700m away with the weapon (Korolkov 2014).

By now, we have a sense of how the SVD is used both physically and tactically, and little about that picture has changed as we bring our story up to the present day. What *has* changed, however, is the battlefield contexts in which the SVD has been used, and how the SVD is facing up to a new age of highly sophisticated sniper weaponry. In the following section, therefore, we will evaluate the impact of the SVD largely through the 'War on Terror', fought primarily in Afghanistan and Iraq between 2001 and 2021, and the scattering of civil wars that have blighted many countries and regions since the start of the new millennium. Doing so enables us to see that the true impact of the SVD, in much the same way as the AK assault rifle, lies as much in the scale of its distribution as in the way it is made and handled.

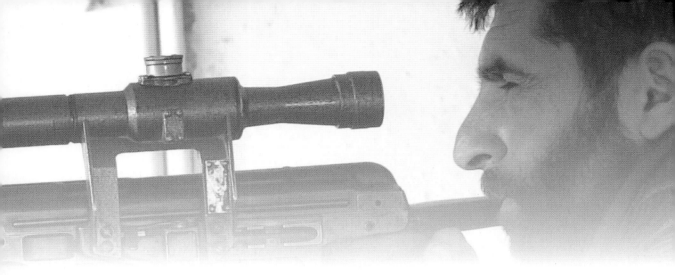

IMPACT
The 'War on Terror' and beyond

A Kurdish PKK sniper takes aim with his SVD rifle. This view shows the PSO-1 side mount to good effect. The scope is released simply by moving to the right the lever between the two sight bracket arms, allowing the scope to slide off to the rear. (Kurdishstruggle/Wikimedia/CC BY 2.0)

Chechnya was just one of numerous conflicts in which the SVD has seen service since the fall of Soviet communism in 1991. In fact, it would probably be quicker to list those wars in which the SVD has *not* been in action over the last three decades. The primary reason for this is that the SVD has been scattered across the world in volumes achieved by few other sniper weapons, if any.

The numbers of SVDs produced by the Soviet Union is unknown, but will certainly number many hundreds of thousands and likely run into the millions. These weapons were distributed widely during the Cold War to various hotspots, where most of them remain active today – properly maintained and stored, an SVD will give decades of service. After the fall of the Soviet Union, the SVD stayed very much in production and development in Russia, with large volumes being sold to export customers as divergent as Bolivia and Burundi. China's Norinco arms manufacturer has added its own versions of the SVD to the global stockpiles. The combination of massive SVD distribution during the Cold War and continual production since then has ensured that the SVD is the most prolific semi-automatic sniping rifle in modern history, and possibly the most widely used sniping rifle since the end of World War II.

In terms of its impact, here is where the SVD makes an historical intersection with the AK-47 assault rifle and its derivatives. As an individual weapon, the AK-47 has little to separate it from most other assault rifles manufactured since the 1960s, possibly with the exception of its legendary reliability. Where it has excelled, however, is in its mass distribution globally. We could make the same argument for the SVD. Many articles and studies of the SVD highlight its limitations as a sniping weapon, particularly when it has to reach beyond ranges of about 600m. In most cases, I would not argue with that assessment; but if we start to

This Russian Army paratrooper sniper was photographed in 1995 while undertaking winter training before deployment to Bosnia. The photograph shows how the SVD can be 'winterized'. With the restrained application of proper lubricants, the SVD will operate reliably even in severe sub-zero conditions. (Georges DeKeerle/ Sygma via Getty Images)

include the mathematics of production and distribution, the picture begins to change.

If we plotted SVD snipers on a graph of talent, the bell curve would show the typical bulge and concentration around the average. Because of the SVD's distribution figures, however, the numbers of those who could handle the rifle with genuine skill might still outnumber the entirety of those professional snipers issued with an optimal but rarer and more expensive sniping rifle. Viewed through this lens, the stories that crop up of SVD snipers taking shots out to 1,000m and beyond actually might not be cases of sheer luck, but in some ways could be the logical outliers of mass distribution.

I would argue that three factors in particular give the SVD its impact: its functional accessibility as a sniper platform (I'm including the PSO-1 sight in this equation); its tactical flexibility across a practical combat sniper range (c.200–800m); and its widespread distribution. All of these points can be clarified within the context of the wars of the 21st century,

The SVD has been exported to several South American countries during the Cold War and post-Soviet eras. These Bolivian Navy snipers, wearing their full camouflage ghillie suits, are on parade in 2008. (Israel_soliz/ Wikimedia/GFDL)

57

The SVD (top) in modern polymer furniture is here displayed next to an SVDS folding-stock variant designed for use by airborne troops. In addition to the folding stock, the SVDS rifle is shortened by switching to a stubby flash hider. (Vitaly V. Kuzmin/ Wikimedia/CC BY-SA 4.0)

where we have seen the SVD serve not only as a sniping weapon within professional armies, but also, like the AK-47, become a weapon of choice for insurgents and terrorists.

IRAQ, AFGHANISTAN AND SYRIA

The wars fought in Afghanistan and Iraq between 2001 and 2021 have been modern proving grounds for the SVD as a DMR and as a sniping rifle. As in the wars in Chechnya, SVD snipers during this period have often faced off across the battlelines. In Afghanistan, for example, the SVD was in use with both the Afghan National Army (ANA) and the Taliban they fought; similarly in the case of the Iraqi Army in its wars against the various insurgent groups that flourished following the Coalition invasion in 2003, including al-Qaeda and Islamic State. From a Western perspective, however, the most pressing point for military commanders and tacticians has been the impact of SVD sniping on US, British and other Coalition forces.

In Afghanistan, although the Taliban acquired and used all manner of stockpiled, bought, captured and stolen weapons, the SVD has been one of the most common sniping rifles, not least because large numbers of ex-Soviet rifles remain within the country and because Afghanistan and neighbouring Pakistan have been hubs for trade in ex-Cold War weaponry and more modern firearms. Around 2009, an SVD would have cost only about $1,500–$2,000 to purchase on the open market in Afghanistan, a fraction of the cost for an advanced Western sniping rifle. (By way of

comparison, an AK-series assault rifle would have cost about $500–$800.)
It is also worth mentioning that the United States funnelled *c*.600,000 small
arms into Afghanistan for ANA forces between 2001 and 2016 and these
included 3,227 sniping rifles and 36,575 further unspecified rifles (Mehra
et al. 2022: 4). As the overall US imports into Afghanistan were weighted
towards Soviet/Russian weaponry, and given the numbers of SVDs in the
hands of insurgent snipers, we can perhaps assume that many of the sniping
rifles were SVDs, now in the possession of the victorious Taliban.

A Taliban sniper, photographed at the beginning of the Afghan War in November 2001. The solid construction and simplicity of function, plus the availability of Soviet-era weapons, made the SVD an ideal sniping instrument for low-logistics groups such as the Taliban. (Scott Peterson/Getty Images)

Given the fact that the Taliban is not the sort of entity to collect or
publish rigorous combat data, the exact operational details and kill data
of Taliban SVD operations are not available. They have, however,
published chilling propaganda videos showing sniper kills, which give
some insight into their tactics and capabilities. The targets they selected
were mostly those of opportunity and tactical carelessness – soldiers
silhouetting their upper bodies above positions of cover or milling around
vehicles; sentries standing bored at outposts; patrols moving through open
terrain. The ranges of the shots vary from about 200m to what appear to
be distances of about 500–600m (although the videos are taken through
a camera, not through the sniper scope). Given that we cannot see the rifle
in the videos, we cannot say for sure that the shots come from an SVD,
but in some instances there are some clear indicators that they do. In one
harrowing video, an individual who appears to be an ANA soldier is
sitting on the back seat of a static Humvee, about 150m away from the
shooter. His body is framed between the open rear door and the door

frame. The sniper takes a shot, and the soldier slumps to one side, wounded but clearly still alive. The sniper pauses momentarily, and then begins sending out rounds at a rate clearly only possibly with a semi-automatic rifle. In this way he makes sure of his kill.

The impact of the SVD on Coalition and ANA operations in Afghanistan was locally significant. In an article entitled 'Did a Dragunov Change the Nature of the Insurgency in Afghanistan?', Robert Beckhusen explains how US soldiers operating with the 2d Battalion, 503d Infantry Regiment, were affected by suspected SVD sniper kills in 2009 that spread fear and operational paranoia among them. The concern was specifically attached to the possibility of the sniper having an SVD, rather than any other form of weapon, which was likely because the SVD gave the Taliban a reach and accuracy not provided by their standard AK assault rifles (Beckhusen 2021).

The impact of the SVD in Afghanistan also went the other way, however, in that the ANA equipped its own snipers with SVDs. Occasionally, even Western troops took them into combat. One of the most famous SVD actions in Afghanistan occurred on 3 October 2009, when the isolated Combat Outpost Keating in Kamdesh District, Nuristan Province, was attacked by some 300 Taliban insurgents, the outpost garrison being outnumbered nearly 3-to-1. In an astonishing action, the US and ANA forces managed to hold off the day-long attack, although it would cost them 14 dead and 27 wounded. During the battle, Staff Sergeant Clinton Romesha, a section leader with Bravo Troop, 3d Squadron, 61st Cavalry Regiment, 4th Brigade Combat Team, 4th Infantry Division, took up an SVD that had been dropped by an ANA soldier. With this rifle he proceeded to take out an enemy machine-gun crew and three Taliban insurgents who had managed to penetrate the outer perimeter of the base. Clearly the semi-automatic functionality and intuitive operation of the SVD meant that Romesha was able to use the firearm effectively, despite the fact that it was essentially an improvised weapon for the US soldier. Romesha's astonishing actions on the day of the battle (most of which are not described here) led to his being awarded the Medal of Honor.

The other theatre in which Coalition forces faced the impact of the SVD, or at least its Al-Kadesiah variant, was Iraq. Although improvised explosive devices (IEDs) became the single greatest threat to Coalition troops following the invasion of Iraq in 2003, snipers also inflicted a heavy toll on troops. One analysis of 100 consecutive British combat trauma casualties who sustained wounds between 1 January and 1 October 2006 found that gunshot wounds accounted for 24.4 per cent of the total (Ramasamy et al. 2009). Most of the sniping incidents took place in urban settings, environments that provided the insurgent snipers with both plentiful cover and avenues of approach and escape, but also limited the ranges of engagement and therefore the demands on their skills as snipers. This was ideal territory for the SVD.

Reports and feedback from Coalition forces in Iraq began to express increasing concern about the growing threat from snipers from c.2005. Award-winning journalist Christopher John Chivers was embedded within US Marine Corps units in Iraq in the mid-2000s. In one of Chivers' articles for *The Orange County Register* in November 2006, the

This Kurdish Peshmerga soldier hedges his bets tactically by equipping himself with an AKM assault rifle, fitted with an extended magazine, in addition to his sniping rifle, which appears to be an SVD rather than the Iraqi Al-Kadesiah. (Kurdishstruggle/Wikimedia/CC BY 2.0)

commander of the 2d Battalion, 8th Marines, explained that he had had eight sniper strikes on his soldiers in eight months (two of the men died) and that the situation was getting worse. Chivers explained that by and large the snipers demonstrated 'unexceptional marksmanship' (Chivers 2006) and tended to take their shots within 300yd (274m), often using SVD-type rifles. Although the snipers' shooting skills were strictly average, their tactical skills were improving to compensate. The snipers would apparently work alongside a network of civilian spotters, helping the snipers to identify the most vulnerable targets – most of their shots were taken when the US troops were not actually engaged in combat. The snipers' choice of firing positions was also intelligent. They would take maximum advantage of the complexities of the urban environment, one in which they usually had the advantage of local knowledge. They would operate from well-concealed positions, such as within rooms inside buildings or from cars fitted with special shooting ports, then disappear quickly into the labyrinth of streets and buildings once they had taken the shot. Alternatively, they might fire from the opposite side of canals or similar obstacles, to slow down the US forces' combat response. At their most ruthless, a sniper might also fire from a position among dense groups of civilians, preventing the US troops, mindful of 'collateral damage', from responding with heavy return fire.

It is impossible to quantify the impact of snipers in Iraq with formal data, but all the reports from the field testify as to how the presence of an SVD-equipped sniper generated as much fear and operational caution as it did casualties. Some insurgent SVD snipers achieved high status during the conflict, and one semi-mythological figure from the war in Iraq between 2005 and 2007 stands out. He was known simply as 'Juba', an insurgent sniper serving with the Islamic Army in Iraq. In 2005, a video was posted online purportedly showing Juba sniping US soldiers in Anbar province and southern Baghdad. The video content, accompanied by the haunting soundtrack of *nasheeds* (a popular form of vocal music in the Islamic world), is graphic. In each of the clips, only a few seconds long, a typically relaxed US soldier is shown, at distances ranging from what appears to be under 100m out to many hundreds of metres. Sometimes the soldier is walking out in the open, his full body on display, whereas in others the soldier is hunkered down in an armoured vehicle, only his helmeted head visible to the outside world. In each case, a shot sounds and the soldier slumps to the floor or recoils from the impact. More videos of the increasingly legendary Juba were released in 2006 and 2007, one apparently documenting 37 of his supposed kills, and even showing a brief image of the man himself. Other claims have his kill count as high as 143 US service personnel.

There is a real possibility that Juba is an invention of propaganda. Details about the man are shadowy and incomplete, and sceptics argue that the videos are simply composites of many different sniper shootings – but the reality of Juba was certainly taken seriously by US soldiers operating in Iraq during this time. On 5 August 2005, the UK's *Guardian* newspaper posted an article by Rory Carroll headed 'Elusive sniper saps US morale in Baghdad', with the subheading 'Commanders weigh their options as "Juba" notches up more kills' (Carroll 2005). The soldiers interviewed by the newspaper certainly felt intimated by Juba's presence, the 1st Battalion, 64th Armor Regiment, based at Camp Rustamiyah in Baghdad crediting Juba with the killing of at least two members of the battalion and the wounding of six more. His *modus operandi*, according to the US troops, was to target dismounted soldiers or those stood up in a Humvee turret, aiming for gaps in their body armour, particularly around the lower spine, ribs or head. His field craft was also impressive. He never took more than one shot so as to avoid revealing his position, and demonstrated both exceptional patience and also resistance to US counter-sniper efforts to draw him out. Analysis of the videos for ABC News by former Green Beret sniper Major John Plaster, one of the world's foremost authorities on sniping, led to Plaster stating that whoever the sniper was he showed 'judgement and discipline', taking a single clear shot before escaping the scene. 'This is not a zealot; this is a calculated shooter' (ABC News 2006).

The weapon used by Juba is somewhat up for debate, based on the grainy images that are meant to depict the man and his rifle. One of the images appears to show a Tabuk Sniper Rifle, an Iraqi weapon that looks similar to the SVD but is actually a modified version of the Yugoslavian 7.62mm Zastava M70 assault rifle. Other images, however, clearly show the sniper with an SVD or at least the Iraqi Al-Kadesiah variant. One clue as to the weapon is that a video message allegedly from Juba himself declared that he had 'nine bullets' in his rifle, and he intended to kill nine people with them. The Tabuk Sniper Rifle's distinctive curved magazine holds 30 rounds, whereas the SVD and Al-Kadesiah magazines each hold ten; the Iraqi sniper likely only loads nine to avoid placing the magazine spring under undue pressure, which might lead to misfeeds.

What seems clear from the combat experience of Iraq, is that the SVD provided insurgent snipers with a perfect means to extend the range at which they could inflict attrition, but also with a platform that could compensate for their shortcomings as professional snipers. Video footage of Islamic State snipers firing at Kurdish Peshmerga soldiers in Kirkuk, Iraq, in 2017, for example, shows them typically using their SVDs to take

The ongoing Syrian Civil War is another conflict in which the SVD is the primary sniping weapon. These two Free Syrian Army fighters are using Romanian PSL rifles in an attempt to shoot down a government helicopter circling above Khan Sheikhoun, Syria, in May 2012. Like the SVD it closely resembles, the PSL has achieved wide international distribution, both to commercial and to military customers. (Austin Tice for The Washington Post via Getty Images)

A Russian sniper operating in Syria in 2017 poses with his SVD. This particular grip, with the front arm braced against the chest to provide a solid vertical support for the rifle, is especially practical when wearing bulky body armour, as the armour provides more depth and rigidity for the arm to rest against. (DOMINIQUE DERDA/AFP via Getty Images)

shots at 200–400m, a very comfortable range for the SVD and for even the most basically trained marksman. It is also observed that the snipers frequently used tracer rounds, possibly to facilitate shot adjustment but equally likely because tracer rounds show the shot trajectory for the benefit of propaganda videos (Miles 2017).

UKRAINE AND BEYOND

The impact of the SVD, based purely on its deployment and use in modern-day warfare, is unquestionable. We cannot deny, though, that in modern armies the SVD is starting to show its age, and that its importance in the future might be limited. This has become evident in the conflict between Russia and Ukraine, prior to and following the Russian invasion of February 2022.

In 2014, the Donbas region of Ukraine was struck by an uprising of pro-Russian separatist groups, which global security agencies quickly recognized as including Russian troops and special forces and mercenaries on the Russian payroll. The pre-invasion conflict between the separatists and Ukrainian armed forces, in both its mobile and static phases, has been to a large extent a sniping war. On the Ukrainian side, one battalion commander estimated that 80 per cent of his losses in 2020 were from

Chambering 12.7×108mm ammunition, the KSVK/ASVK sniping rifle is one of a new breed of large-calibre anti-materiel sniping rifles issued to be found in increasing numbers among Russian forces operating in Ukraine. (Vitaly V. Kuzmin/ Wikimedia/CC BY-SA 4.0)

A pro-Russian sniper, dressed in full ghillie suit, sits in a car while guarding the front entrance of Lugansk's regional administration building on July 2014. (DOMINIQUE FAGET/AFP via Getty Images)

The SV-98 emerged in the late 1990s in Russia, designed at Izhmash by Vladimir Stronskiy. It is chambered for both 7.62×54mmR and 7.62×51mm NATO ammunition. With its heavy free-floating barrel and precision bolt mechanism, it has been rated at 1.15 MOA at 100m by Russian special forces. (Vitaly V. Kuzmin/Wikimedia/CC BY-SA 4.0)

Russian snipers (Plaster 2022). In return, Ukrainian snipers imposed equally heavy casualties on the separatist troops. One of the Ukrainian snipers with a high public profile is Olena Leonidivna Bilozerska, a woman in her 40s turned sniper, with at least ten kills in the Donbas to her name. Bilozerska's weapon of choice is the SVDM rifle fitted with a thermal scope for night-time shooting.

Sniping has equally been a central feature of the outright war between Russia and Ukraine since February 2022. Several very high-ranking Russian commanders have been killed by Ukrainian snipers. They include Major General Andrei Aleksandrovich Sukhovetsky, deputy commander of the 41st Combined Arms Army of Russia's Central Military District, killed on 2 March by a sniper apparently firing from a distance of 1.5km (the range almost certainly rules out the use of an SVD rifle, however). Ukrainian snipers have also preyed heavily upon Russia's badly manoeuvred and frequently static supply columns, picking off drivers and soldiers fleeing from trapped vehicles, and using anti-materiel sniping rifles to disable vehicles. In return, Russian snipers have been equally active, particular against Ukrainian fixed positions in the east and in the city battles to the west. The death of one Russian sniper, Junior Sergeant Sergei Igorevich Tsarkov, 38, a leading military sniper and international shooting competition winner, in April 2022 hit the international headlines.

The SVD has continued to make an impact in the conflict in Ukraine, but we also see its influence weakening. In the early years of the conflict from 2014, SVDs were used heavily on both sides. Yet while the Russian forces included professional snipers equipped with SVDs that had high-quality ammunition, new barrels and modern scopes, the cash-strapped

Ukrainian troops often had SVDs with worn barrels, ageing PSO-1 scopes and very limited supplies of precision ammunition; when this ammunition ran out, they had to resort to firing standard infantry ball rounds (Zimmerman 2020). To make matters worse for the Ukrainians, the Russian snipers were highly trained and professional, whereas the Ukrainian military scarcely had the expertise or the stocks of ammunition for advanced sniper training.

Then came the matter of weaponry. From 2017, the defence press began to report on the official Russian military replacement for the SVDM – the Chukavin SVCh developed by the Kalashnikov concern. Like the SVD, it is a gas-operated semi-automatic type that can be chambered for 7.62×54mmR ammunition. In fact, it can even take the SVD's ten-round magazine. There, however, the similarities end and modernity takes over. The internal mechanism is essentially an accurized version of Kalashnikov's

A Ukrainian sniper takes aim through his SVD at a checkpoint near the town of Popasna in Lugansk region on 2 October 2014. The cloth wrapping around the barrel and forend provide a measure of camouflage plus cushioning to stabilize the weapon when it is rested on a solid support, such as a wall or window frame. (ANATOLII BOIKO/ AFP via Getty Images)

A Russian sniper in 2016 contemplates his next shot while his SVD cools off to one side. The Russian Army and security services have invested heavily in sniper training over the last decade, sniping being a cost-effective force multiplier. (Нацгвардія України/Wikimedia/ CC BY-SA 2.0)

rotating bolt allied to a short-stroke gas mechanism. Its features include: a 410mm cold-hammer forged free-floating barrel; ambidextrous firing controls; a collapsible buttstock adjustable for length of pull, with adjustable cheek riser (the top of the buttstock is set straight in line with the top of the receiver); a full-length Picatinny rail on the top of the receiver and a short rail beneath the plastic forend, the lower rail taking a folding bipod; and ten- or 20-round magazines. Most significant is that the rifle is available in alternative chamberings, specifically 7.62×51mm NATO/.308 Win and .338 Lapua Magnum (8.6×70mm). Compared to the SVD, the Chukavin SVCh is an altogether more modern package, and shots out to 1,000m and beyond are well within its capabilities.

Aside from the Chukavin SVCh, however, Russian special-forces snipers have also been using a wide variety of Western bolt-action and semi-automatic sniping rifles, plus the domestically produced Orsis T-5000 bolt-action type, which can be chambered in five different calibres ranging from 6.5×47mm Lapua through to .375 CheyTac. Another powerful Russian bolt-action type is the SV-98, introduced in 1998 and combat-tested in Chechnya, chambered in .308 Win, 7.62×54mmR and .338 Lapua Magnum. Russia has also invested heavily in anti-materiel

rifles – often repurposed for anti-personnel use – with exceptional ranges in excess of 2,000m. (Note that tests with the .375 CheyTac in the Orsis T-5000 in 2019, for example, saw Russian snipers putting rounds on target at 2,000m.) The key types are the 12.7mm ASVK, configured in a compact bullpup arrangement, and the lightened ASVKM. The Russians are also fielding the semi-automatic OSV-96 in the same calibre, with a free-floating barrel, integral bipod and five-round magazine. This weapon is capable of engaging infantry up to 1,800m and vehicle/materiel targets up to 2,500m. Fitted with the latest optics, the new generations of Russian rifles have begun to muscle out the SVD, offering superior performance over ranges the SVD simply cannot match reliably. Russian forces in Ukraine still utilize the SVDM and SVDK in significant numbers, however, mainly within front-line infantry units engaging the enemy at closer ranges. The capabilities of the modern SVD have also been improved by better scopes, such as the 3–10× 1P70 'Hyperion' optic, but in Ukraine the SVD is steadily becoming far less influential within Russian forces than it would have been had the conflict been fought a decade previously.

On the Ukrainian side, the prevalence of the SVD is also steadily being diluted by new generations of more advanced and longer-range sniping weapons, to keep pace with the weapons in Russian hands. Since 2017, the Ukrainians have received significant supplies of Western sniping rifles, chambered for calibres used by the NATO countries – Ukraine is evidently looking towards greater integration with the West in terms of military materiel. Examples of the weapons supplied include the M24 Sniper Weapon System (SWS – essentially a military version of the bolt-action Remington Model 700), the Savage 110 (another bolt-action type) in .338 Lapua Mag and several .50-calibre anti-materiel rifles, including the Barrett M107A1. More significant in terms of the relationship with the SVD, Ukraine has also produced its own semi-automatic sniping rifle, the

This sniper of the Russian National Guard special forces is conducting a training exercise near the nuclear power plant at Novovoronezh. He is armed with the shortened SVDS, with its noticeably shorter flash hider. (Mihail Siergiejevicz/SOPA Images/LightRocket via Getty Images)

A Ukrainian soldier from Ukraine's Territorial Defence Forces patrols a residential district in Mali Prokhody, Ukraine, in September 2022. The fact that he is armed with an SVD could mean he is operating more in the Designated Marksman role, as the majority of Ukraine's snipers are now equipped with more advanced Western rifles. (Viacheslav Mavrychev/Suspilne Ukraine/JSC "UA:PBC"/Global Images Ukraine via Getty Images)

UAR-10, that signals a complete shift away from the SVD model. It is based on the Armalite AR-10 operating mechanism and is chambered in 7.62×51mm NATO. The rifle has a 508mm chrome-lined free-floating barrel, an aluminium receiver, a Magpul PRS-style buttstock, a Picatinny top rail and a lightweight configurable forend. Feed comes from a detachable box magazine, either ten or 20 rounds. Crucially, the UAR-10 is designed to take accurate shots consistently out to 1,200m, outstripping the *c.*800m effective range of the SVD. By 2019, some 600 UAR-10s had been issued to Ukrainian troops. The Zbroyar concern that manufactures the UAR-10 has also produced a precision bolt-action sniping rifle, the Z-008, chambered in options of seven popular calibres, from 5.54×45mm to .338 Lapua Magnum.

Based on the Armalite AR-10 rifle rather than a Soviet-era weapon, the Zbroyar UAR-10 is beginning to replace SVDs in Ukrainian military and law-enforcement use. (VoidWanderer/Wikimedia/ CC BY-SA 4.0)

THE MIDDLE GROUND

The situation in Ukraine illustrates that although the sun has not yet set on the SVD in professional armies, the venerable rifle is steadily being eclipsed by types that deliver more range, better ergonomics, modular flexibility and more power. Looking at the situation globally, however, we will surely see the SVD remain in combat service for many years and possibly decades to come. This is not only because the SVD has been significantly improved in its more modern variants, but also because of the tactical position it very convincingly occupies.

In 2009, a contributor to the forum on the website snipershide.com posted what might initially appear as an uncontroversial question: 'What is the average military sniper shot distance?' The word 'average' triggered some quite argumentative responses, especially from those who claimed that the well-trained sniper did not work with the concept of 'average' at all, being prepared to shoot across the full spectrum of the weapon's effective range. Such was the nature of the debate that the poster was even compelled to change the wording of the question to the less incendiary 'At what distance are military sniper shots taken?' (Snipershide.com 2007).

The host of the discussion noted that while the average shot distance for law-enforcement marksmen/snipers is available, and is very short (figures in the range of 50–75m), data for military snipers appear largely excluded from the public domain. This is understandable in some ways, as it would be useful information for actual and future enemy combatants. But there were some interesting replies from former military personnel. One individual related his personal experience, likely from Afghanistan or Iraq, stating that company snipers generally took shots in the 50–250m bracket for urban operations and 200–400m for countryside environments. Another contributor referred to Peter Senich's two works *Limited War Sniping* and *The Long-Range War: Sniping in Vietnam*, both of which give the figure of 430yd (393m). The consensus of opinion from the forum was in the region of 400m, however.

A Bangladesh Army sniper takes part in the 'Sniper Frontier' competition round of the 2021 International Army Games at the Mieu Mon National Training Center in Hanoi, 31 August 2021. The standard Bangladesh sniping rifle has been the Chinese Type 85, although the country's military is now gravitating towards more advanced Chinese models. (NHAC NGUYEN/POOL/AFP via Getty Images)

An Indian soldier uses the PSO-1 optical sight on his SVD to scan the terrain from his position overlooking the Indian Army barracks in Gingal Uri, some 90km north of Srinagar near the Line of Control between India and Pakistan, following a December 2014 attack by militants in the area. (ROUF BHAT/AFP via Getty Images)

OPPOSITE
The Indian Army purchased thousands of SVDs for the Designated Marksman role in the 1990s. Since 2018, however, reported problems with inadequate long-range range accuracy, particularly in the contexts of border clashes with Pakistan and anti-terrorism operations in remote, mountainous areas, have spurred efforts to replace the SVD with more advanced sniping weapons. (ROUF BHAT/AFP via Getty Images)

There is some mathematical quibbling underpinning this debate, principally about whether we are talking mean, mode or median average. Really the hunt is on for the mode average, the most common range at which sniper shots are taken, as the outlying extremities of sniping distance at each end of the scale will likely skew the median and the mean. The general point is understandable, however. Although snipers can and do take shots out past 800m, 1,000m and even beyond, such shots are rare and not representative of the most common combat ranges.

This fact does have a bearing on our understanding of the impact of the SVD. The SVD does not recommend itself as a weapon with which to take shots out to 1,000m and beyond, but within the range spectrum in which snipers (not just DMs) most commonly work it has been a weapon of genuine influence in a huge range of conflicts. A sniper and his operational success are much more than just the output of the theoretical accuracy of his weapon. A good sniper will learn the idiosyncrasies and the pros and cons of his rifle and work around and with them to maximize the potential of the weapon through good technique and field craft. Choices include scope set-up, cartridge choice, stock adjustments, maintenance regime, barrel support, grip and breathing technique. Such decisions, plus the general expertise of the shooter, can turn an average weapon into an excellent one, at least when measured by battlefield success.

The final compelling factor that will ensure the SVD continues to have an impact on future battlefields is, as already noted, that it is out there in the world in large numbers. While professional armies in highly developed countries will be unlikely to stick with the SVD, if they haven't transitioned out already, the SVD will still be a weapon of choice for insurgencies, armies of developing nations and anyone who wants a weapon that can dependably put shots on target out to 800m and occasionally beyond.

CONCLUSION

A soldier of the Iraqi Army's 75th Brigade fires his SVD at a zeroing range at Camp Taji, Iraq, on 28 September 2016. The photograph was taken just as the bolt reached the rear of its travel under the force of gas pressure, the spent cartridge case being ejected through the side port. (Cpl. Craig Jensen/Wikimedia/Public Domain)

In any overarching assessment of the SVD, we have to keep in mind the reason for which it was designed and whether that rationale is still relevant to the modern military marksman or sniper. An answer might be found in an article by Charlie Gao in *The National Interest* magazine on 28 June 2021, titled 'Russia's Killer: The Dragunov Rifle Is Beautiful Just the Way It Is'. Gao convincingly outlines how the SVD, when it first entered service, was one of the most advanced and compelling sniper packages in the world. Gradually, the SVD has been technically overtaken by new generations of rifles coming into service, despite some efforts to the modernize the rifle for the new era; but the SVD, even in its original form fitted with the PSO-1 scope, remains one of the world's most popular sniping weapons, still giving lethal service in almost all of the world's war zones.

Gao proffers two explanations as to why this is so. The first is that in contrast to the Western model of the independent, roaming sniper, separate from the main body of troops, the SVD was conceived as a way to improve the power and range of the squad, a role that it does perfectly. The second is that it has followed a similar design philosophy to Kalashnikov's AK-47 – it is basic, reliable and simple to use. These qualities mean that as long as a shooter has been given essential training in the use of rifle and scope, and has acquired tactical fundamentals, the SVD will provide him with an accessible tool of the trade, one that is relatively inexpensive but perfectly capable of killing people at extended ranges.

The technologically advanced, and extremely expensive, sniping rifles we often see in the hands of elite Western snipers are the pinnacle of the mechanical art of rifle design, and generally equip those given the best training available. We have to recognize, however, that on the bell-curve distribution of global sniping, these individuals and weapons sit at the upper extremity. At the thick middle of the curve are snipers armed with

rifles like the SVD. They might not be the best shots, and they might not have the optimal equipment, but in the same way as the AK-47 changed the global security landscape through its broad distribution, SVD-armed snipers are a disproportionate presence on many modern battlefields.

As we have seen, the presence of a sniper, even if his or her shots are rarely fired, can dominate the daily lives and operational movements of major units. Soldiers operating in an area known for snipers have to move constantly under cover and concealment, inhibiting the speed at which tasks and missions can be performed, as well as enduring the mental stress of knowing that sudden death could arrive at supersonic speed, from angles and positions unknown. Whether the specific type of rifle adds anything to this fear is debatable, but in summarizing the battlefield impact of the SVD we can say with some confidence that lives will continue to be taken by this weapon for decades to come.

A sniper from the Nagorno-Karabakh Defence Army's 8th Regiment runs to take up position against Azeri snipers in May 2004, along the front line of the disputed territory of Nagorno-Karabakh in Azerbaijan. The SVD is an ideal weapon for such positional warfare. (Jonathan Alpeyrie/Getty Images)

BIBLIOGRAPHY

ABC News (10 February 2006). 'Baghdad Sniper: Myth or Menace?' https://abcnews.go.com/WNT/story?id=1604797

Alexiev, Alexander (1988). *Inside the Soviet Army in Afghanistan*. Santa Monica, CA: RAND.

Beckhusen, Robert (2021). 'Did a Dragunov Change the Nature of the Insurgency in Afghanistan?' *The National Interest*: https://nationalinterest.org/blog/reboot/did-dragunov-change-nature-insurgency-afghanistan-194324

Bolotin, David Naumovich (1995). *Soviet Smalls Arms and Ammunition*. Hyvinkää: Finnish Small Arms Museum.

Carroll, Rory (2005). 'Elusive sniper saps US morale in Baghdad.' *The Guardian*: https://www.theguardian.com/world/2005/aug/05/iraq.usa

Chivers, C.J. (2006). 'Riflemen use Iraqi civilians as spotters and shields.' *The Orange County Register*: https://www.ocregister.com/2006/11/05/riflemen-use-iraqi-civilians-as-spotters-and-shields/

Defense Intelligence Agency (1982). 'Tactics, Training, and Equipment.' *Review of the Soviet Ground Forces* (DDB-1100-364-82). Washington, DC: Defense Intelligence Agency, pp. 14–23.

Dragunov.net: http://www.dragunov.net

Forgotten Weapons (2019). 'History of the SVD Dragunov with Max Popenker' (video): https://www.youtube.com/watch?v=eDhEOQPaDu0

Fortier, David M. (2004). 'Russia's New 7.62×54R Sniper Load.' *Small Arms Review*: http://www.smallarmsreview.com/display.article.cfm?idarticles=2017

Gao, Charlie (2021a). 'Russia's Killer: The Dragunov Rifle Is Beautiful Just the Way It Is.' *The National Interest*: https://nationalinterest.org/blog/reboot/russias-killer-dragunov-rifle-beautiful-just-way-it-188789

Gao, Charlie (2021b). 'Chinese Sniping Rifles: A Brief Introduction.' *The National Interest*: https://nationalinterest.org/blog/reboot/chinese-sniper-rifles-brief-introduction-198234

Gebhardt, Major James F. (1997). *The Official Soviet SVD Manual: Operating Instructions for the 7.62mm Dragunov Sniper Rifle*. Boulder, CO: Paladin Press.

Grau, Lester W. & Cutshaw, Charles Q. (2002). 'Russian Snipers in the Mountains and Cities of Chechnya.' *Infantry*: 7–11.

Korolkov, Alexander (2014). 'Devastating in trained hands: The Dragunov sniper rifle.' *Russia Beyond*: https://www.rbth.com/defence/2014/06/30/devastating_in_trained_hands_the_dragunov_sniper_rifle_37811.html

Mehra, Tanya, Demuynck, Méryl & Wentworth, Matthew (2022). *Weapons in Afghanistan: The Taliban's Spoils of War*. The Hague: International Centre for Counter-Terrorism.

Miles (2017). 'Threat Analysis: IS Marksmen in Kirkuk.' Thefirearmblog.com: https://www.thefirearmblog.com/blog/2017/04/17/threat-analysis-marksmen-kirkuk/

Onokoy, Vladimir (2021). 'The Last of the Dragunovs.' *Small Arms Review*: https://smallarmsreview.com/the-last-of-the-dragunovs/

Plaster, Major John L. (2022). 'Sniping in Ukraine.' *American Rifleman*: https://www.americanrifleman.org/content/sniping-in-ukraine/

Ramasamy, A., Harrisson, S.E., Stewart, M.P.M. & Midwinter, M. (2009). *Annals of the Royal College of Surgeons of England* 91: 551–58.

Senich, Peter R. (1977). *Limited War Sniping*. Boulder, CO: Paladin Press.

Senich, Peter R. (2007). *The Long-Range War: Sniping in Vietnam*. Boulder, CO: Paladin Press.

A US Army sergeant observes Ukrainian soldiers exiting a BTR armoured personnel carrier during a live-fire training exercise at the International Peacekeeping and Security Center in Yavoriv, Ukraine, 12 November 2016. The three slots on the side of the forend indicate that this rifle might be of 1960s or 1970s vintage. (Sgt. Jacob Holmes/Wikimedia/Public Domain)

Snipershide.com (2009). 'At what distance are military sniper shots taken?' Posted by natesfitness: https://www.snipershide.com/shooting/threads/at-what-distance-are-military-sniper-shots-taken.8634/

Thomas, Timothy L. (2005). 'Russian Tactical Lessons Learned Fighting Chechen Separatists.' *Journal of Slavic Military Studies* 18.4: 731–66.

Thompson, Leroy (2022). 'Russian 7.62×54R SVD Sniper Rifle'. *Tacticallife.com*: https://www.tactical-life.com/firearms/russian-762x54r-svd-sniper-rifle/

Vilchinsky, I.K., ed. (1984). *Mastavleniye po stralkovumu delu-7.62mm snayperskaya vintovka Dragunova (SVD)* [Manual for operating the 7.62mm Dragunov Sniper Rifle]. Moscow: Military Press of the Ministry of Defence of the USSR.

Vorobiev, Marco (2011). 'Guns of the Spetsnaz. Part II Sniper rifles: the wide-open spaces of Afghanistan were made for sniper warfare, and the Soviets made good of the SVD sniper rifle.' *Shotgun News*: www.thefreelibrary.com/Guns of the Spetsnaz part II sniper rifles: the wide-open spaces of...-a0247740939

Walter, John (2017). *Snipers at War: An Equipment and Operations History*. London: Greenhill.

Zimmerman, Vera (2020). 'The Role of Snipers in the Donbas Trench War', *Eurasia Daily Monitor* 17.26: https://jamestown.org/program/the-role-of-snipers-in-the-donbas-trench-war/

INDEX